France Speaking

By
ROBERT DE SAINT JEAN

Translated from the Original French
BY
ANNE GREEN

1941
E. P. DUTTON & CO., INC.
NEW YORK

FIRST EDITION

AMERICAN BOOK—STRATFORD PRESS, INC., NEW YORK

TO THE REPRESENTATIVES
OF THE PRESS AND OF THE RADIO
OF THE UNITED STATES
WHOM I SAW AT WORK DURING
THE WAR

FOREWORD

This is not just one more narrative of the drama which France lived in 1940.

During the war I jotted down in a notebook the encounters, reflections and memories which had any connection with the fate of my menaced country.

My record ends on June 17th, after the resignation of the Reynaud cabinet, which truly marks the end of an epoch; it is simply the unpolished record of an average Frenchman who belonged to no party and who, as a democrat, was brought to confess bitterly the mortal sins of his democracy.

In reading over these pages, it seemed to me that they might perhaps hold a permanent interest on account of the light they throw on the relationship which exists between democracy and the butter and cannons which Hitlerism has made so tragic, not only for France but for many other great nations. "To be or not to be" is the dilemma that has been imposed upon the modern world by Germany under this form: "Cannons *or* butter." The French democracy, through the voice of her leaders, answered first: "Butter," then "Butter *and* cannons," and to-day almost nothing is left to her, neither butter nor cannons, nor democracy.

How we could have reached such a pass is impossible to explain without going back in time, without discovering that the final catastrophe was merely the result of mistakes made during the weeks, months and years which preceded it. Some assure us: "We lost the war on June 10th." Others reply: "No, on May 13th." In reality the war was lost before the war: our political, diplomatic and military misconceptions had silently settled our fate before the first cannon shot was fired. Modern defeats are primarily determined in inefficient bureaucracies, in over-garrulous parliaments and in somnolent munition plants.

Proofs come to us unceasingly from France that the French of today wish to know the reasons for their misfortune. And the French of tomorrow will no doubt be even more impatient than those of today to know the whole basis of the catastrophe. During this war, as in every war, France experienced what the slang of 1914 called the "bourrage de crâne." Literally, this means the stuffing of brains with boosting, fallacious hopes. Before this war of 1939 she allowed herself to be lulled with illusions, and this has cost her dear. Now, we want the truth. Truth is not the pretty lady which legend portrays for us, gracefully rising from a well, mirror in hand. No, we have been fooled about truth: it is a terrifying monster. Happy people cannot look it in the face, they would lose all desire to eat, drink and be merry; and that is why they avoid it, preferring to gaze on someone else whose name is "Wishful Thinking." This last person has an infinitely more pleasing aspect. But France, who has looked defeat

in the face, who has looked the invader in the
face, who has looked humiliation in the face,
who looks famine in the face, can gaze face to face
on truth without dropping her eyes. But it is im-
perative that the French master themselves, that in
finding the explanation of their tragedy, they do not
seek out motives for further pitting themselves one
against the other. Those who, from party spirit, lay
all the blame upon the opposite party, do not serve
their country nor the truth—but Adolf Hitler.

Nevertheless, one need scarcely say that the necessary compiling of errors and culprits cannot lessen
or diminish France in any way. It is true that many
men in office, many leaders, have proved unworthy
of their trust, and that these leaders were chosen by
the average Frenchman, who thus has his share of
the responsibility. But to denounce political, military or moral errors does not in the least imply the
general decadence of France. A contribution as magnificent as that of France between 1918 and 1939 is
one of which any country can be proud. France has
but one thing to regret: that, as Paul Valéry once
said, before the war, her politics were not on the
same high level as her thought.

Each and every one of us must work to make it
otherwise tomorrow. Anyway, there is only one way
to bear the present and to escape the obsession of
the past, and that way is to turn to the future, to
think about the time when, delivered from that most
punctual "collaborator," the Nazi vampire, we can
take back the exclusive direction of our destiny.

Even if, contrary to our hopes, England does not

win the war, this day must come in spite of everything! We do not yet sufficiently realize that the two words "Future" and "Liberty" have become synonyms and that France, who has just passed through the Good Friday darkness of her history, will inevitably attain her Easter Sunday.

We were wrong in being behindhand but we have not been the slowest among nations. We were grievously wrong in not considering the German menace even more seriously than we did, but others realized even less clearly than we that the Nazi storm would surpass in violence all such scourges registered by History.

The storm has not yet ceased its ravages, and that is why the free countries which still remain in the world can teach themselves more than they suppose by learning how our democracy ended in such disaster. Not that all democracies are alike or that what took place in one should inevitably happen to another. It would not be honest thus to simplify the question. The French democracy had taken a shape and had contracted diseases which were hers only. . . . However, the ordeal inflicted upon it is now, and will continue to be, inflicted on others. It is only too true that the faculties of resistance and adaptation of all modern democracies are actually being submitted to a terrible experience from the double attack, internal and external, of the Nazi microbe. And all the democracies in the world possess a certain number of faults in common as well as a certain number of good qualities. And it is well to throw some light upon these common faults, upon the germs of death which democracy bears in its bosom as do all existing political regimes. Heaven knows what price the French have paid for this discovery: may the lesson at least not be lost; may each of us profit by what Hitler has taught us in order that we may more surely get rid of Hitlerism.

New York, 1941.

FRANCE SPEAKING

PARIS

———————

TODAY I had lunch with Paul Reynaud at the Ministry of Finance. The war has changed nothing in the atmosphere of the building; the ushers still wear that air of crushing superiority which they evidently owe to the fact that they are sure of keeping their jobs for fifty years, whereas the minister can be sacked at any moment. . . . In the enormous office where he presides over the management of the French Treasury, Paul Reynaud appears more diminutive than ever, and in spite of myself I am reminded of caricatures where Sennep, our best cartoonist, depicts him as Mickey Mouse. . . . However, he holds himself up at his full height, and his extraordinary vitality is not lessened by his staggering daily overwork. He keeps the same bantering, mocking manner, the same vivacious expression, the same keen glance, the same swiftness of thought. He could easily pass for ten years younger than his real age, which is sixty-one.

"Well, things have taken a new turn since I saw you. . . ." He says these words with the bitter irony of a Cassandra whose predictions have come true. The "new turn" of events—the war—had been announced by Paul Reynaud for years, and as early as 1937 he used to repeat: "We are at present in the bloodless period of the war." Last July when I came to interview him for *Paris-Soir,* Paul Reynaud said to me: "As Minister of Finances, I am obliged to continue giving out the watchword *Business as usual,* so as not to alarm French production, but I am certain that the 'business' cannot continue for very long 'as usual' because Germany *cannot* wait any more and will surely make war very soon." I remember most clearly the circumstances of our meeting; the engine of the plane which flew us from Paris to Le Touquet hummed resoundingly. As we could not make ourselves heard in the din, Paul Reynaud had scrawled his answer on a sheet of paper. . . . And a few months earlier, in November 1938, he had already told me: "Munich does not delay the danger of war, quite the contrary. For now, not only are the Reichswehr and the Nazi party fully agreed, but the generals themselves are pushing the country towards the war-adventure so as not to allow the favorable moment to escape them. At this moment Germany possesses an enormous advantage in armaments over France and England. . . ." And that very day he had showed me a letter which he had just received from London and which echoed his words. This letter was signed by Winston Churchill.

We had no lack of predictions, and many other Frenchmen besides Paul Reynaud pointed a warning finger towards the approaching storm, notably two of our ambassadors. However, it was the opinion of most of our ministers that their reports were written by alarmists. . . .

After signing a few papers, Paul Reynaud rose, saying gaily: "And now to lunch"; he guided me towards the dining-room through a labyrinth of passages and stairways such as can be found only in our ministries. He walked quickly, with the short step of a *chasseur alpin,* almost a run. General Giraud, one of our greatest hopes as army commander, came in soon after us, followed by the Minister of Blockade, and Monsieur Pernot, and the President of the French Bar.

As thirty-nine Communist deputies have just been arrested, and measures against ringleaders in the factories are announced, the Communist problem was discussed. This is a delicate problem to solve in a country at war and, what is more, it has been difficult to understand properly since the signing of the German-Russian Pact in August, 1939. The General Confederation of Labor and the Socialist party had taken a position against the pact, and a great number of adherents to the Communist party had sent in their resignations as members of that party. But the greater part of the latter did not, on that score, decide to become Socialists, so that there remained an important mass of workers whose opinions were not known. These workmen kept an attitude of reserve, some through confusion of mind, some from reasons of prudence and a certain number because they could not nerve themselves to anathematize leaders in whom they had put their trust only yesterday. . . . Meanwhile the work in the factories continued satisfactorily, with very few exceptions, but a great many agitators who before the pact had done Stalin's job now worked for Hitler and secretly diffused the theme of German propaganda: "The Nazis defend the true Socialist cause, making war against capitalism and the Two Hundred French Families." [1]

The measures taken by the government are variously appreciated and Reynaud lets it be understood that he considers them far too mild.

"Daladier will not take a firmer decision," he says dryly.

Once more, one feels resentment in one's voice on behalf of the man who preaches energetic policies but who sees the favor of the masses go to those who do not ask too great an effort from them. The antagonism between Daladier and Reynaud is most interestingly explained: it is that of the average Frenchman for the Frenchman who cannot be placed in a conventional pigeonhole, that of the lusterless provincial for the Parisian lawyer, that of the party leader for the free lance, etc. . . . There are people who belong to the singular species, others who belong to the plural species, a man was heard to re-

[1] The "Two Hundred French Families" were the propaganda theme of the Communist party for the elections of 1932 and 1936. According to Communists, the policy of France was occultly directed by two hundred bankers, manufacturers and other capitalists, all to be counted in the ranks of our bourgeoisie. And they were two hundred, not one more, nor one less.

N.B. *The notes at the foot of the pages, the extracts from the conversation between Paul Reynaud and "Curiosus" in 1936 and the list of the French cabinet, have been added to the original text.*

mark one day. Well, Daladier is of the plural type while Reynaud belongs to the singular. And to the most singular species, at that.

This is all the more curious as, in Reynaud, careful dressing, derby hat, pelisse, pearl tie pin and the background of his life all show him up as a conventional bourgeois. But under these appearances hides a person with a very decided leaning towards nonconformity. He has a thirst for official honors, he certainly secretly hopes one day to become President of the Republic and at the same time, he disconcerts, he embarrasses, he takes risks, as much in his private as in his public life. By his boldness he alarms those whose consideration he covets, by the biting tone of his remarks he chills the noisy popular assent which he so much desires to hear rising around him.

When he denounced the timidity of the government in the affair of the Communist leaders, I recalled an anecdote which he frequently related to visitors: "The other day, I proposed a bold measure to the Council of Ministers. Daladier said nothing. One of my colleagues opposed my project. Daladier still said nothing. . . . Once more I took up my plea and my colleague took up his. Followed an embarrassing silence and Daladier understood that at last he must commit himself. So he put on a fierce expression, knit his brow, banged on the table with his fist and cried: 'Gentlemen, let us compromise!' "

After speaking his mind about rulers, Reynaud did not spare those whom they governed: "The morale is not what it ought to be," he began by declaring; "people complain about the scarcity of coffee. On all sides, deputies, associations, electors write, asking me to remedy this state of affairs! Well, is this the time to give our currency to South America for a little more coffee, currency which we can better use during war time by purchasing arms, machines and planes?"

And he concluded with the following words: "Less coffee will have to be drunk, that's all. And many other privations will have to be endured. If I had my own way, there would already be three meatless days a week. . . ."

Reynaud then asked me what was happening in the United States—I had returned ten days before from America. That country has always interested him and he has made numerous visits to it. He speaks highly of the Chief Executive as he has been created by the American Constitution.

"We have nothing of the sort in our country," he says, "and that is most unfortunate."

How many times have I heard political men in my own country deplore the extraordinary weakness into which authority has fallen there! And in these men this opinion is not always dictated by party spirit, for many leftist leaders are, in private, no less vehement on the subject than are the conservative representatives of the right wing. Of course they carefully choose their audiences before expressing these regrets and only most exceptionally do they inform their constituents on this subject. But it is nevertheless strictly true that between themselves these auguries do not conceal the defects of the regime, and the lobbies of the Chamber are, contrary to what might be expected, among the spots on French soil where the encroachments of the legislative over the executive powers have often been clearly denounced by "connoisseurs."

Reynaud next spoke of armament bonds and of the broadsides which he intends to post on the walls of Paris, to arrest the attention of potential subscribers.

"The drawings shown me were too tame, too conventional, so I preferred to present great photographs of tanks and planes. The French are seldom given an idea of French strength and yet this, if ever, is the time to do so. Silhouetted on these posters they will see modern tanks, of which we have so few and for which I have clamored for years. . . ."

As lunch progressed, I was much struck by the frequency of Reynaud's exclamations: "I have so often said so! I told you so! I was right!" This "right and righteous" turn of mind, so common in politicians, was not a marked characteristic of his in normal times. Certainly the past has shown him sometimes as boastful, with a peremptoriness exquisitely irritating to Daladier. . . . But I had never noticed in him as I did today the obsession for proving that he had seen rightly and the others wrongly. It cannot be his single and passionate desire to become prime minister which moves him to show his clearsightedness to the detriment of his competitors; it is something else which I cannot quite discern but which leaves me profoundly uneasy.

And now he relaxed a little and joked with General Giraud, a companion of his youth. Together they had sat on the benches of the Lycée Louis-le-Grand.

After this interlude, Hitler's plans were discussed and one of us expressed the opinion, a very prevalent one nowadays, that the Führer would attempt to wear us out by long months of inaction, so as completely to sicken us of this war. A great many people believe that this is the latest and most perfidious invention of German propaganda. For the French, who loathe war, wish to fight when war has become unavoidable and detest nothing so much as being mobilized "for nothing." As early as September, popular opinion could be heard expressed in every street by the following refrains: "This time, it's got to be finished once and for all." . . . "We're sick of all this blackmail and these crises coming up every six months." . . . "Since he insists on having it so, we're going to make *him* see reason."

"I don't in the least believe," said Reynaud, "in a wearing-out war."

General Giraud approves of the Minister of Finances' remark and says that his own information has brought him to the same conclusion.

"In any case," one of us continues, "nothing will happen until the spring."

"That is not certain," replies Reynaud, "the Germans may attempt something against our front and that maybe before Christmas. They had not anticipated a Franco-British declaration of war, so at present they are readapting their plans. . . . But when their new decision is taken, and their preparations finished, they will strike hard and quickly. And they will strike at us. . . ."

When the general had left, Reynaud said to us: "He is made for initiative and fighting, he is the most amazing 'battle animal' that I have ever encountered. . . ." And he recalled the general's astonishing adventures during the 1914 War.

General Giraud, who was then a captain of the Zouaves, was seen to fall on the battlefield during the Charleroi retreat in August, 1914. One of his comrades tried to bring him back to our lines but was struck by an enemy bullet and fell on Giraud's body. French officers who witnessed the scene declared that both Giraud and his friend had been killed, so they were reported as dead. Madame Giraud was informed, the captain's cap, sword and canteen were forwarded to her but she refused to believe in her husband's decease. The same evening, Giraud, who had only fainted, came to, found himself a prisoner of the Germans and was interned in a small French village. A few weeks later some peasants gave him an old suit of civilian clothing and he escaped. He pretended to be a Belgian and for some time things went pretty well for him. Then he was unmasked and recaptured. In November, he succeeded in escaping once more, in the company of Schmitt, another French officer. They disguised themselves, Giraud as a stable lad, then as a coal heaver, Schmitt as a dishwasher in a restaurant. While plying their new trades, they accumulated information concerning enemy activities and troop movements. A smuggler disguised them as carpenters and helped them to Belgium. But once there, how to live? Giraud obtained a job as juggler in a traveling circus. Then he heard that someone was coming who would help him into Holland. This someone arrived and Giraud recognized him as a deserter from the Foreign Legion. The two men took a liking to each other and Giraud said to the legionnaire: "From now on I shall never leave you; if you try to get away from me, I'll shoot you down like a dog. . . ." But the legionnaire scrupulously kept the promise he had made to help his erstwhile officer and Giraud finally reached Flushing, whence he sailed to England, then back to France. . . .

Today, Giraud commands a reserve army corps, the Seventh Army, and some men in Reynaud's circle see in him a future commander in chief who will end the war victoriously. For the impression is that Gamelin will not remain long in office. . . . The general opinion, among the "well-informed," is that the Generalissimo is intelligent but has a weak character. This is currently translated by the brief remark: "Too much of a politician." But this verdict is not without appeal, for the same sentence was, I believe, passed on Joffre before the 1914 War. In any case, I feel myself incapable, as indeed the immense majority of my compatriots are, of appraising a general. . . . The High Command is something sacred to us, something on which we dare not cast critical eyes, for to do so we would have to possess a technical competence which is not ours, and because, since the victory of 1918, the respect which we entertain for the General Staff excludes all skepticism. The French, who have the reputation of unceremoniously doubting most things and most people, have, during the last twenty years, considered General Headquarters taboo. This is so true that the leftist parties which, before 1914, noisily expressed their antimilitary spirit, now, during sessions at the Chamber, chime in with the Conservatives to applaud when allusions are made to the General Staff. The voting of military credits no longer provokes the tumultuous scenes of the past. For years and years the High Command has pretty nearly had *carte blanche,* and this is cause for hope among those who, from other motives, feel uneasy. To put it differently, two Frenchmen out of four have confidence in Daladier (a legendary Daladier, very dissimilar to the real Daladier) but four Frenchmen out of four believe in the French Army.

OCTOBER 10TH

Yesterday at the Quai d'Orsay I saw R. who informed me that in the forty-eight hours which preceded the declaration of war, the Minister of Foreign Affairs and the Prime Minister separately asked General Gamelin once more if France were in condition to fight. General Vuillemin, commanding the Army of the Air, recalled the weakness of our aviation, but General Gamelin concluded that in spite of this, we could fight. In 1936, at the time of the Rhineland reoccupation, Gamelin, when his opinion was asked, had replied that a general mobilization was necessary if we wished to show a military reaction to the German initiative.[1] In 1938, just before Munich, the French commander in chief had said in London that he believed it possible to break through the Siegfried Line, and gave the cost of the operation. But the frightful backwardness of French aviation (and also of British aviation) at that time had stopped the Allied Governments on the path of intervention. In 1936, from information gathered *a posteriori*, Nazi Germany still was bluffing and her generals followed Hitler against their wills at the most hazardous point of his career. The German Army, impossible as it sounds, went to the borders of the Rhine without any serious preparation having been made for its return, and much confusion ensued before it was properly quartered. There were also many errors in execution, but of smaller importance, during the invasion of Austria; I remember, on the road to Linz, in March, 1938, seeing an entire motorized column at a standstill; it had broken down. In September, 1938, Germany was no longer bluffing. During the weeks which preceded

[1] This total mobilization, said Paul-Boncour later, would have been "obviously disproportionate to the event, no matter how serious. This mobilization could have been wholeheartedly and unanimously accepted by the nation *only if it had been convinced by full evidence that this supreme sacrifice was unavoidable.*" It is as if Monsieur Paul-Boncour had said: "when a fire has broken out in a house, one must not call in the firemen before persuading all the tenants that it is necessary to do so."

the Munich Conference, many among us thought that a gigantic poker party was in progress between governments. But, two months later in Berlin, it was proved to me that if Paris and London had not given in, the war would have been on. It seems that in the weeks following the Munich Conference, Hitler often regretted to his intimates that he had not made war.

In September, 1939 Germany was bluffing no more than she was in 1938. Those in authority must know this, and if the Generalissimo said that we were in a position to fight, it must mean that we have partly caught up with our arrears and have seriously increased our chances during the months which have elapsed between the Czecho-Slovakian crisis and the Polish crisis.

When I attempt to determine clearly my reasons for hoping in victory, I cannot help asking myself at the same time if those (and they are very numerous) who believe that the war will end in a stalemate are right. This opinion about a stalemate is prevalent, so prevalent that one even surmises to what extent it is the result of Nazi propaganda. For Nazi agents continue their work in our country. At any rate, this opinion is the outcome of the Nazi policy that has been directed towards us for several years past and is, above all, the fruit of Munich. For after Munich, the average Frenchman believed with his whole heart that Hitler would threaten him but did not desire a war. Cunning people have invented a "French version of Hitler," far less dangerous than the original version: of course a gangster, but crafty as a Parisian peddler, preferring blackmail to slaughter.

These last few days, mysterious peace proposals from the Führer have been much talked about. Only last week, some people at a table next to mine in a restaurant conversed about these proposals for at least an hour, and when a little later I went to buy stamps at the *bureau de tabac,* the same kind of conversation was rife in the adjoining bar. And the identical talk buzzed in buses and the underground. Hitler's speech of October 6th has put an end to these illusions but they slumber at the bottom of many a heart.

On the boat which brought me back from New York last month, I remember meeting a lady from Metz, a very good, patriotic Frenchwoman and mother of a large family. "I am going home," she said, "but this war can't last, something will be *arranged.*" She added that she never read the papers but that she had heard of an approaching mysterious agreement (for that is what she meant by "arranged"), through a message sent by some relatives in Switzerland and these relatives had correspondents in Germany. . . .

Stranger still, as soon as I reached my barracks, regimental comrades repeated the same information, almost word for word, adding: "And it's going to be *arranged* before Christmas, you'll see!" They continued confidently: "The proof is that *he* has not bombed Paris; so that must mean that he has some idea at the back of his head." In short, one of the characteristics of this *drôle de guerre* is that it is

waged by soldiers of whom a great many do not believe that there will be a war—and this at a time
when they are at war.

In the Champs-Elysées, trenches, which are called
shelters, have been dug, but this scarcely changes the
appearance of the avenue, where almost as many
cars race up and down as in peace time. Along the
arcades of the Rue de Rivoli war sticks its nose into
shop fronts—but with elegance, thanks to the paper
arabesques glued to the glass panes. A few stores are
closed, their show windows sleeping behind iron
shutters; on the latter one reads a small hand-written
sign: "Closed because of mobilization." At the door
of a merchant of "Souvenirs and Watercolors" another sticker says this: "He is somewhere in France
but I can show you what he painted before leaving.
Signed: The artist's wife."

There are faded flowers lying before Joan of Arc's
statue, just as in peace time. But there are nosegays
before the statue of Clemenceau—and this is like war
time. In the Place Vendôme, an elegant woman
alights from an elegant car to disappear into an
elegant dressmaking establishment; this is like peace
time. But two Scotch officers, light switches in hand,
enter a shop in the Rue de la Paix; this is like war

time. Maxim's is full, just as in peace time, but sand-
bags are piled over the foot of the obelisk on the
Place de la Concorde and this decidedly means war
time.

If certain statues have been concealed under sand-
bags against eventual bombardments, others have
not been protected. Those which remain exposed to
view are those which are not worth seeing. Everything of any value is hidden; the sandbag has become the symbol of artistic merit.

As to the blackout, it is not absolute. The *Ville
Lumière,* as Paris used to be called, is not extinguished. Might I say that she has merely put on
dimmers? At first the obscuration was almost as strict
as that of London, then a few liberties were taken
and at these the authorities winked. It seems that
Paris, in spite of semiprecautions, can still be seen
from a plane at a distance of some sixty kilometers.[1]
But no one thinks much about this. At barracks, a
comrade made a bet with me that not a bomb would
fall on the capital. He is a mechanic from Montmartre and chance has put him in the same office
with me. As we have very little work to do, I have
plenty of time to listen to his reflections and sallies.
From time to time we are given *livrets militaires* [2] to
bring up to date. So we go on indefinitely writing in
large round characters that the possessor of each *li-
vret* has obeyed the mobilization order, or, as the set
military jargon has it: "Was called back to activity

[1] About thirty-seven miles.
[2] *Livrets militaires* are the papers which each Frenchman carries regarding his military duties.

on September 3, 1939." My soldier from Montmartre finds this sentence extremely funny: "Why say that we have been *called back* to activity the day we joined the colors? Would that mean that as civilians we are all sluggards?"

It is only in France that every soldier examines each word he meets, without allowing himself to be dazzled by incongruous terms.

"And when we're demobilized," pursued my comrade, "how will they put that down in our *livrets?*"

"We'll write," answered the sergeant: " 'Has rejoined his hearths' ". (*Ses foyers,* which means hearths as well as homes in French.)

"His *hearths!* Why put it in the plural? Does the army think that we keep up two or three establishments apiece?"

Yesterday, my pal said: "Tonight, I will listen to the radio, for 'Dala' is speaking." To decide beforehand to listen to a prime minister and above all to abbreviate his name with affectionate familiarity is a rare sign of popularity. This is all the more flattering as Arthur (this is my pal's name) passes for a rather *forte tête,* that is, he is somewhat hard-boiled. He used to read *l'Humanité* (a suppressed Communist paper) and now falls back on *l'Oeuvre. Paris-Soir* because it is amusing and *l'Oeuvre* because since the last war this paper has had the reputation of not going in for too much bamboozling and *bourrage de crâne,* are the two favorite daily papers among soldiers.

If one tries to understand why Monsieur Daladier exists as an important entity for Arthur and his fellows, one reaches the following conclusion: The Prime Minister pronounces firm, dignified words which satisfy popular patriotism but at the same time he does not inflict too stringent penances on his compatriots. Thus each one is openly happy to hear his virile accents and privately equally delighted to keep to pretty much the same life as in peace time.

Our modern vocabulary classes political men as "hard" or "soft." Well, Monsieur Daladier has a hard gaze and a soft hand.

In addition to this he is the victim of a photographic art which portrays him with little reference to reality. This is true of more than one popular personality among our contemporaries. But in Monsieur Daladier's case, the travesty is extremely marked. In the public eye he becomes a sort of gloomy, distrustful bull, whereas he is really an anxious, hesitant animal.

After hearing the head of the government's speech, Arthur nodded his head approvingly; he agreed with the energetic words which he heard and at the same time, he finally owned to me, he persistently believed that there was some way to put an honorable end to the conflict. "Dala" would not allow the opportunity to escape him, when it comes along, he asserted. "But," I say, "everything was attempted, *before the war,* to stop the catastrophe and it couldn't be done. . . ."

"That's true," answers Arthur, "and I even thought that something would be wangled at the eleventh hour to get Poland out of her mess. Of course, everybody has known for ages that there would be a tough time coming this summer, but everyone on Rue Notre-Dame-de-Lorette (the street in which he lives) thought that we could wiggle out of it without too much of a rumpus."

And that is why, my companion next explains, the mobilization was carried out amid astonishment or skepticism from most of the mobilized men. "And then, it is no longer enough nowadays to shout: 'A Berlin,' as in 1870, in order to believe that something has really happened. War is a tough job now," he concludes. It is certainly true that the men left for the front with admirable discipline—but silently. The *Marseillaise* which was heard from every village when the men left in 1914 was not sung this time. There was no singing of any kind.

Last night, when dining with some friends, we tuned in on the Stuttgart radio. Attacks against the English, demonstrations of friendship for the French ... etc. .... There is nothing subtle in this program, therefore it is specially well-adapted to reach the majority of listeners. After the traitor's voice, the silky accents of the distinguished female traitor of the station is lifted in an appeal to French mothers, all in the very best taste. But I forget to mention the principal point: at the beginning of this charming little festival, Traitor Number One (for there are two male traitors) had said: "The war was not in the least unavoidable, we could have come to terms with you in the course of a conference. . . ." And all of a sudden, I recognized some of the sentences which flavor the conversation of Arthur and his peers. Very few of these men have heard the Stuttgart broadcasts, but German propaganda has reached them through other channels and above all, *has been battering away at them for years, without their being aware of it.*

We should have defended ourselves against this invisible weapon also; we should have built a Maginot Line against such methods of aggression; better still, counterattacked. But our political system is essentially opposed to this. In principle, a democracy is a regime where every voice has a right to be lifted; consequently the enemy's also has a right to be heard.

And at the same time, dictator-ruled Germany's absolute censorship suppressed everything that did not tally with the Nazi plan and point of view. So we were prevented from pleading our cause and the cause of peace.

If, in the past, certain of our papers have expressed opinions which in the long run favored German interests, others denounced the ideas at the back of Hitler's mind. But one and all, in giving front page importance to the smallest scraps of information concerning the Führer, indirectly worked for Doctor Goebbels' department. "I don't care whether the notices I get are favorable or hostile, so long as I get them! That's the only thing that counts!" exclaimed one of our playwrights not so very long ago. . . . Well, before the war, our dailies all played their part in the enormous concert of publicity which has contributed so vastly to Hitler's success. This publicity has given life to a skilfully manufactured picture of Germany's leader, and that for the benefit of millions of Frenchmen who would have been incapable of remembering the least detail concerning their own chief executive.

I recollect that in 1938 Monsieur Daladier had the happy idea of sending in secret for the heads of newspapers and asking them to give less prominence to Chancellor Hitler's declarations. The editors promised to show more discretion but did not keep their word. And a few minutes ago, unfolding my evening paper, my attention was arrested by an enormous headline running across the front page: "What Is Hitler Going to Do Now?" Censorship, which needlessly suppresses so many things, allows Frenchmen—in full flight of war—to read headlines of such size that they are at once led to think that "the gentleman across the way" (who has sworn their destruction) is a person of such importance that his decisions can change everyone's destiny.

On each of my trips to Germany during the past few years I noticed that the "publicity allowed to the State" took up more and more room. This is not a Nazi invention, it is a law of dictatorships, but modern scientific methods have never yet been utilized on the massive scale adopted by the Third Reich for its celebrated "launchings." For the sufferings of the "oppressed brothers of Austria" were "launched"; also the "Jewish misdeeds," the "tortures of the Sudetens," etc. just as X's tomato juice or Y's watch are "launched." The Nuremberg Congress with its immense orchestration has been the tom-tom drum for the Nazi doctrine, just as the Automobile Show, on a smaller scale, has been for the automobile salesmen.

In our democracies no publicity is given to any but private enterprises, and we are all perfectly familiar with the names of a manufacturer of furniture, shoes, cough syrup or table knives. But it has never occurred to anyone that the coarse methods of compulsion which characterize commercial advertising might serve the reputation of the State. In consequence, the "Firm of France" has never been advertised, while on the other hand the "U.S.S.R. Firm" and its head "Stalin, the genial father of peoples," the "Firm of Italy" with its "Duce who is always right," the "Firm of Germany" and its incomparable Führer, have been given world-wide publicity amid great din and fracas. And this advertising has also penetrated to our country's heart.

The result of all this, among other things, is that the system which suits the more highly civilized among human beings—our system—does nothing to extend the radiation of its principles of civilization throughout the world. Thus this system loses morally, first of all, the ground which it will next be obliged to abandon economically, diplomatically and then militarily. And if this system does do something to further its prestige, it is by ways and means which have not changed in the last fifty years—and which are accompanied by almost complete ignorance of contemporary technical acquirements. In contrast, the understanding of this new technique is found to a superlative degree among the manufacturers of totalitarian poisons, who shout their own wares.

OCTOBER 14TH

Some Swiss returning from Basel have confirmed a piece of news published several days ago: by mistake, a short while since, a rumor spread over Germany that hostilities were ended. Following this information joyful manifestations had spontaneously broken out in three big cities on the Rhine; restaurant-keepers treated their customers to free drinks, etc. . . . And this brings up the problem of German morale.

The people who took part in these manifestations do not belong to a species born yesterday. For many years, millions of Germans have sulked (this is the least one can say) against the enormous adventure into which they are being led by Nazism; at the same time, millions of other Germans are intoxicated with the idea. After each success of Nazi foreign policy I have been to Berlin or to some other part of Germany and I have always been surprised to see how passively very many Germans of all classes have greeted the news of their latest "triumph." The incredibly unforeseen and surprisingly profitable outcome of Munich did not succeed in permanently galvanizing the whole Teutonic tribe. I pass over in silence the bitter or hostile remarks made to me by Germans who spoke frankly because they had known me before the birth of the Nazi regime. . . . Must one conclude from all this and from the later signs which we have noted since the outbreak of war that the Third Reich will crumble to pieces of itself without some violent blow from the outside? Not at all.

Anti-Nazi Germany, which held so many trump cards, was unable to do anything against the storm troops before 1933 and from year to year the world has awaited an uprising which has never taken place. The only danger of an explosion was grazed in June, 1934 when elements of the Nazi party even more violent than others thought that the rhythm was not rapid enough. . . . These elements were subdued, and as to the "good Germans," they have not budged. They have been conquered by terror, which is (another fact we are apt to forget) a most effective means of government. At any rate, effective in Germany.

The passersby with gray, worried, ill-nourished faces whom I have met on the Wilhelmstrasse or elsewhere all showed, if examined closely, the mournful resignation of prisoners of war. And the witticism that our ambassador to Berlin made one day in 1937 remains profoundly true. Monsieur André François-Poncet was asked to give a definition of the Nazi revolution, and replied (and that before some Nazis who took his answer as a joke): "The Nazi revolution is an operation by which the Germans have definitely become prisoners of the Boches."

As long as we have not inflicted a serious defeat upon Hitler, he will keep his prisoners. However that does not mean that we must not attack, and by

all possible means, the German morale. I wonder
what is being done in this direction, as much in
France as in England, in the way of radio broadcasts
specially designed for Germany, or in the line of
tracts.

OCTOBER 15TH

"The other day," says Arthur, "Gamelin's wife
was asked out to tea. The friends who had invited
her received a fine letter in the General's handwrit-
ing explaining that his wife was too busy to accept
the invitation but that he would be happy to replace
her and even to stay on after tea for a little game of
bridge. . . . So you see," concludes Arthur who loves
this fictitious story, "that this war is not a serious
business!"

OCTOBER 16TH

The press has scarcely mentioned the accord between employers and workmen by which both parties agreed simultaneously and freely last week to
put both their greatest efforts in the output of war

armaments. This "sacred union" of capital and labor was accomplished in the office of Monsieur Dautry, Minister of Armaments.

This means that the working hours are at last to be increased and that we ourselves will no longer be hampered, as in the past, by the social laws which, since 1936, have so decreased the figures of production. In short, we are knocking the shackles from our feet and have decided to run after Germany, who still is several years ahead of us.

In 1938, struck by the general air of overwork and ill-health on Berliners' faces in the poorer quarters, I decided to take a walk in the direction of the Kotbus Strasse and there to do a little marketing. I knew the normal wages of a workman and had been told what part of this sum he could spend on food. By inquiring about prices in various shops I very quickly had proof that the average buyer could for the most part purchase tinned goods (especially herring), sausages, and vegetables (potatoes, cabbage); and this was confirmed by noting what was bought by various women shoppers who came and went under my eyes. Upon my return to Paris I tried to tell about this in an article and was astounded to receive from readers of *Paris-Soir* numerous and duly signed letters of protest; and what is more there were also letters, unsigned this time, couched in most indifferent French and of a threatening nature.

The reasoning of my correspondents—small employees and working people—were as follows: We, ourselves, could not work nine, ten and eleven hours eating so little and so poorly. So they could not put

up with such food any more than we could, so you
are telling us lies. . . .

As I received these letters I understood what the
standard of living of the most modest of my compatriots means to them. . . . So all the speeches about
"Germany which does without butter to have guns"
remained a dead letter for listeners who: *a*. Did not
believe that human beings could almost entirely de-
prive themselves of butter to have more and more
guns. *b*. Imagined that they were being told of non-
existent German privations in order to be prepared
for demands of corresponding sacrifices. *c*. In consequence, were suspicious of such information and did
not believe it.

Today they consent to these sacrifices and agree to
modify somewhat their past way of living: it took a
war to obtain this result. Just as it also took the war
to wring necessary concessions from employers who
were often recalcitrant. Up to the war we cherished
the illusion that we could rearm sufficiently while
keeping to the same standard of living as in the past.

OCTOBER 17TH

The thunderclap of the reoccupation of the
Rhineland on March 7, 1936 had no influence over
the elections which took place a few weeks later. It
was the first time that Frenchmen had voted since

Hitler's accession to power and they insisted on more social reforms, more butter than they had ever demanded during the whole of the French Republic. No doubt the economic crisis, and not foreign policies, influenced their voting. . . . Monsieur Sarraut, who was then prime minister, guessed these reactions like the old politician he was, and contented himself with entering Germany through the channel of the microphone. "We will not leave Strasbourg under the fire of German cannons!" he exclaimed. After which, he went home and the German cannons remained in the positions to which they had advanced. The French prime minister, like Mr. Baldwin in 1935, renounced all energetic action in order to obtain favorable election results. . . . I heard him say to some friends, a few days before the voting, that according to his advices, there would be no appreciable change in the composition of the Chamber and that the Radical-Socialist party would remain, as before, the pivot of French political life. . . . After which a Chamber was elected with the most decided leaning to the left that had ever been seen. Mr. Baldwin had saved, if not his country, his party. But Monsieur Sarraut saved neither one nor the other. The Popular Front was born; expenses between 1936 and 1937 grew from forty-six billions to sixty-four (the increase in the national defence budget was raised by only six billions): the dogma, "butter for all and lots of it" was preached, the forty-hour week decreed at a period when Germany was making cannons twenty-four hours a day *and said so* (Hitler: "Night and day, I have armed the German people.") . . . Certain political leaders were too intelligent not to see the astonishing contrast between the German and French tendencies, but they pretended to believe that it was still possible to have cannons and butter at the same time, and Monsieur Léon Blum subtly declared: "No activity could be more opportune than that which consists in bettering the homes whose defence must be organized."

Unfortunately, the financial policy of Monsieur Vincent Auriol was such that, for instance, if a salary was increased one hundred francs, the cost of living went up in such a manner that these hundred francs did not compensate for the decrease of purchasing power of the sums earned by the working man: the butter melted in the frying pan almost as soon as it was put into it.

In certain cases the generous gospel of butter for all became the excuse, on the part of politicians, for corruption on a grand scale. At Marseilles, notably, abuses became so glaring that, later, the mayor and municipal council had to be discharged from office.

In a few years, the number of functionaries in this big city had been increased by over a third and the town debt had passed from 275 millions to a billion.

The municipal council found it convenient to use for supplementary expenses the assessments which should have been employed in paying off its debts; then it asked financial help from the State, which was already heavily burdened with the armament expenditures.

Even then, if only the money had been spent usefully! But the hospitals and asylums of Marseilles

were the most expensive and the worst kept up in
France. The salaries of the staffs of these establishments had been increased so heedlessly that they finally came to be 30% higher than in Paris. . . . As
there was no single authority, but twenty-five municipal counselors, excesses and abuses multiplied
rapidly without any of those who committed them
having an idea of the total extent of the overbidding
and fraud.

For from overbidding to overbidding the descent
to swindling was easy. An obliging clerk made out
"certificates of indigence" by which the needy are
entitled to necessities, and gave them to one of his
friends who sold these affidavits for twenty francs
apiece. This woman friend was finally arrested and
when she was asked how long she had plied this
strange trade, she candidly replied: "Why, I succeeded my mother. . . ." And when the clerk was also
asked how he had had the nerve to give his accomplice these certificates of indigence, he answered
nobly: "Don't let us go into the matter, I acted from
motives of humanity. . . ."

OCTOBER 18TH

Today it was announced that the detachments of
our troops which had been sent forward to the ap-

proaches of the Siegfried Line had since October 3d been withdrawn to our own fortified positions.

This news has not caused very keen disappointment to the public; it was clear to all that we had undertaken no operations on a big scale since the Polish campaign because we were not prepared to do so. The public had understood without being told that it would be terribly risky to hurl ourselves into a considerable operation with such small aviation forces as we possessed; it was better to finish our general mobilization in safety. The Command heartily congratulated itself on the fact that the enemy had given us time to accomplish this mobilization without a single snag—but, when one reflects upon it, the achievement can only be counted as a negative success. However, they say that "time is working for us," a much-repeated statement which occasions lengthy discussions.

Before the war, Paul Reynaud once said to me: "At the pace we are going, time is working not for us democracies but for the dictatorships." I considered him very pessimistic that day. Since the beginning of hostilities he has slightly modified his statement without making it less striking. "Time is a neutral who will go over to the camp of the strongest."

It is to be hoped that we are doing all that we should to win this ally over to us and that our chiefs have laid precise plans to bring him quickly to our side.

However, while waiting for the war to begin in earnest between the French and German generals, some French generals are making war among themselves; notably, it seems, the Commander in Chief and his presumptive successor General Georges. The news of this struggle first made a bad impression on me; then I reflected that I was undoubtedly foolish to feel any alarm: it was always more or less thus in all armies. A remark made by Marshal Pétain before the war had often struck me, and now again came into my mind: "During the 1914 War," he told me, "I thought that our army was the only one that always had sticks jammed in its wheels, but when I read several years later the memoirs of the German generals, I realized that on their side too their path was strewn with obstacles, that they endured underhand fights from service to service or between the army and politicians. . . ."

OCTOBER 19TH

A journalist went into a school and questioned the children about the war. Here is a dialogue between the reporter and one of the lads:

Q. "Who is the head of the Germans?"

A. "Adolphe."

Q. "What sort of man is he?"

A. "He is a gentleman who does his hair very badly."

Q. "Who is the head of the British?"

A. "The queen, whose name is Elizabeth. She is always smiling and her daughter is also called Elizabeth."

Q. "Who is the head of the French?"

A long silence, then the scholar answers:

"We . . . ell, there are several, some are in plain clothes and the others are in uniform."

The lad's embarrassment shows many things, and in particular that our democracy has tended for too long to become a pure abstraction.

There are several explanations for this: a dread of very strong personalities and—since the famous Boulanger Affair—an obsession for overthrowing the government, in other words, for *coups d'état*. And then, giving way to the rationalistic tendency which is so strong in him, little by little the Frenchman has reduced the government of the nation to a theorem. We are the only country that has ever instituted publicly the cult of the Goddess Reason. One might object that this was an absurdity of the Revolution and that it lasted only a few months. . . . But it is most especially during revolutions that the deeper traits of the national character appear, traits which have remained half-veiled in normal periods. (That Nazi Germany, for instance, should have adored the "Sun and Blood" is no laughing matter; nor can it stand as a picturesque episode, for it is by no means a negligible indication, and it informs us not so much about Nazism as about Germany itself.)

Right, Reason, Justice, our gods, are the noblest

that are, but it is a great pity, particularly in war time, that they cannot in the eyes of the masses be incarnated in some person, and that the crowd should be reduced to adoring capital letters.

Among the presidents of our Third Republic, very few have really "existed" for the average Frenchman. In how many cases have the people known the voice of the president, his familiar gestures, his hobbies and witticisms, his big dog or little cat? At long last, by dint of protecting the citizen against absolute power, the absolute has not only been suppressed, but the power reduced to something negligible; and the men who hold it are transformed into ephemeral shades. . . . For long years the country of Louis XIV has been governed by magistrates who can really say without exaggeration: "I am *not* the State."

There is only one government man whom France has really loved, physically so to speak, in the last thirty years: Clemenceau. He was seventy-seven in 1917 when he saved his country—and that country afterwards showed him the door. Poincaré, Doumergue, enjoyed the esteem of the well-to-do, Briand the admiration of lovers of eloquence, but this cannot be called popularity.

The inconveniences of this state of things are perhaps limited in peace time, but the way is paved to very serious consequences in time of war, as we may observe right now. For with us, a citizen does not really discover the primacy of the State until times like these. As a consequence of the very long historical evolution which has made of him a more

highly civilized animal than most inhabitants of the
European continent, the average Frenchman has
placed politics in quite a secondary rank. Another
people who have been slowly refined by the centu-
ries, the Chinese, also show contempt or indifference
for things touching government. Peace might be defined by Frenchmen, whether they live in town or
country, as "a time when one need not think about
politics and politicians"—politics *a priori* seeming
unclean to them and politicians dishonest. Our
Third Republic has been, during the past few years,
the only country in the world where the appearance
of the Chief Executive on the motion picture screen
can unleash peals of laughter. Most of us think, in
the bottom of our hearts, that politics claim only an
intermittent attention from us, like the tax-collec-
tor's income sheet or an automobile insurance policy
—all of them tedious, unavoidable formalities which
must be dispatched as quickly as possible. What
really counts, what possesses shape, color, weight,
warmth and life, is a field, a garden, a wife, children,
the vineyard and a house, bread and wine, books,
family furniture, Sunday lunch, a church, a school,
the little café on the square, a plough horse, a shop
neatly furnished and stocked, the hoarse old dog and
the old cronies, etc. . . . Every four years the elections take place and of course everyone discusses them
for hours and hours and even argues fiercely with
the neighbors, but the event is considered with secret
detachment. No doubt certain people make a living
out of politics, beginning with the owners of *bistrots;*
and far too many electioneering agents trump up

certain profitable transactions to the detriment of honest people. But how remedy this? These parasites have been accepted as one of nature's minor plagues. If the members of Parliament and the Government have become so mediocre in recent years, the principal reason, at core, must be that politics do not interest the French sufficiently to make them want to rid themselves of such and such undesirable politician. And it took the Stavisky scandal to make the nation thoroughly indignant. Whether the leaders of the right wing, the center or the left were discussed, their names brought the same smile to the lips of those who heard them; all parties showed the same skepticism regarding men in politics. To be fair, many held firmly to certain principles, but only in the abstract. A Communist would not have died for *le camarade* Thorez, leader of the extreme left; and no reactionary would have laid down his life for Monsieur Marin, head of the Conservatives.

War being a time when citizens must contemplate dying for their country, Frenchmen have been brought to realize that they will be killed for Monsieur Lebrun. Now, honest Monsieur Lebrun does not "exist" for them. So it remains to sacrifice one's life for ideas and certainly for very generous ones; but these ideas would have more appeal to the masses if they materialized in the shape of flesh and blood entities, to be known, loved and followed. . . . *La Patrie,* "one's country," is a principle, but it is also a voice, a smile, a living countenance. . . .

OCTOBER 21ST

On leaving barracks, I ran to the offices of my paper, where my comrades made much fun of my uniform; I must say that my garments are so ill-cut that I present the elegant profile of a barrel. It is a pleasure to see those associates of mine who remain, but I feel sad not to be at my profession, working as I used to. . . . I met Jerome Tharaud[1] in a corridor; he is just back from Strasbourg and describes the fantastic appearance of that city, where everything remains as it was, minus the inhabitants. Pots of flowers are still on windowsills, manikins behind show windows mount guard over the shops and gaze sightlessly at streets where not a soul passes; cats play in the middle of deserted thoroughfares. It is as though a wicked fairy had struck the town with her magic wand and put it to sleep.

At the same time, thousands of Alsatians and Lorrainers have been evacuated to the southwest of France as rapidly and as efficiently as possible within narrow limitations. Among other things, there are not enough blankets to give them, and I believe, by the way, that there is not a sufficient quantity for the soldiers. The reason: when France opened her

[1] A celebrated author, who, with his brother Jean, has written a great number of travel and history books and a few novels.

frontier to seven hundred thousand Spaniards who sought refuge in the country after the collapse of Catalan resistance, all the army and Red Cross blankets were taken for the use of the fugitives.

It is not sufficiently realized that the war in Spain has greatly accentuated a mixture of populations which, beginning years ago, has taken the proportions of a migration unprecedented in our history. White Russians, anti-Fascist Italians, anti-Nazi Germans, Austrians deprived of a country, Czechs driven from their fatherland, Poles escaping massacre and disaster, have all found shelter in our country, along with the Spaniards just mentioned: the total refugee population amounted to nearly four millions. No country in the world has shown itself more hospitable than ours.

This evening, saw M. who worked at the Quai d'Orsay until 1938 and afterwards was sent abroad by his adversaries who accused him of having "egged the country on to war" at the time of Munich. Once more I talked with him about Munich.

His attitude is not in the least what certain newspapers have attributed to him. Several years before Munich, he had risen against the policy which led to it, which is quite a different matter. And, after Munich, he protested against those who chose to see it as a sort of success, when in reality we suffered the most humiliating of diplomatic defeats.

I remember that after Munich all the French journalists who were present at the conference returned to Paris in dismay. And Daladier, in the plane which brought him home, imagined that the crowd which gathered at the airport was there—to stone him. When he heard their acclamations, he accepted them graciously (a minister never refuses that kind of present) but once back in the Ministry of War, he murmured, pointing to the crowd which still cheered him: "The fools!" During the following days the misunderstanding grew; a parade headed by the Prime Minister filed by the Arc de Triomphe. This made Monsieur Mandel more indignant than anything else. By chance I met him a few hours later. "We have suffered the greatest catastrophe in our history since Sedan," said he, "and this is no reason to hang out flags and celebrate. When a man meets a gangster who relieves him of his wallet, the victim does not go home celebrating the holdup as one of the happiest events in his life. . . ."

The French naïvely believed that the Munich agreement strengthened the chances of peace. (Nothing is more erroneous than the legend of the cunning Frenchman; we are extraordinarily ingenuous, at least politically.) So the French imagined the Germans to be like themselves, that is, having a horror of war and preferring an advantageous compromise to a bloody struggle. And like Mr. Chamberlain they believed that the signing of the treaty meant "peace in our time." Ah! how many times have we wrangled with the journalists over this question: "Should the Munich agreement have been signed or not?" At the time, many among us were opposed to it, but little by little, as they learned of the terrible gaps in our armaments, they came to think that nothing else could have been done. This does not signify approval of the "appeasement" policy in principle. Not at all.[1] The culprits are those who preached and practised the policy of appeasement three, four and five years *before* Munich. The farther one moves back into time the greater the responsibilities appear. . . .

It would seem that an unlucky spell had been continuously influencing us to do everything at the wrong time and, especially, to make concessions at a time when we possessed forces superior to those of Germany and could have compelled her to moderation. In 1934 and 1935—later on, Dr. Goebbels cynically admitted this—the Nazi leaders trembled continually, for they knew that if France and England summoned the Third Reich to stop its secret rearmament, the Nazi regime would crumble to pieces —forsaken, to begin with, by its army. A year before Hitler came into power I remember visiting Professor Bergstraesser at Heidelberg. He did not openly admit that he was a Nazi, but he nevertheless insisted upon the fact that this party had been able to inflame youth and provoke extraordinary zeal and devotion . . . Herr Professor spoke to me with candor. "The Nazis will take over the government, that is certain," he said, risking a prophecy which many other non-Nazis, and notably Stresemann, had also made. He added: "What bothers me is that, swept on by their own rhythm, they may declare war *too soon.*"

[1] The truth is that we were already doomed at the time of Munich, we had to face either a diplomatic disaster or a military defeat. And in September 1939 a new Munich (advised by Mr. George Bonnet) would not have prevented a total disaster a little later.

This frankness surprised me, simpleton that I was. And I showed myself even more of a simpleton in afterwards believing other Germans who protested that a war such as that foreseen by the eminent professor was unthinkable.

Indeed, logic has not been a constituent of the line followed by French diplomacy during the last twenty years. This line was a mixture of several successive policies, sometimes adopted simultaneously, an ensemble of contradictory ideas and movements which had only one character in common: pettiness. At bottom, neither the policy of junction nor that of resistance was adopted; the result was that we had none of the advantages of a defined attitude but merely the inconveniences of all the attitudes. The reason is easy to find: a bold policy in one direction or the other signified, for a parliamentary leader, such responsibility and such possibility of downfall, that he could not entertain the idea. So the reaction of a minister was to follow a short-sighted, small policy, to put off great decisions, to dodge in and out of obstacles and to follow the stream. It was the policy defined by Berthelot, then General Secretary for Foreign Affairs after the last war. He had been asked which direction had been chosen by the Ministry of Foreign Affairs and replied: "That of the dead dog floating down stream." [1] The dead dog has a good excuse for not choosing its way. But what about our ministers?

[1] The *chien crevé* or "dead dog" policy is well-known in French politics; it means a policy with as many ideas, initiatives or directing energy as a dead dog floating down a river could possess.

If we had made war instead of signing the Munich agreement, would we have had a chance of winning it? That is a question one cannot answer. . . . And another interrogation mark rises in my mind: If we declared war in September, 1939, surely that signifies that we have acquired means which we did not possess in 1938. I believe in the wisdom of our military chiefs.

And if we had given in once more on September 3, 1939, France would soon have become Germany's vassal, a sort of Slovakia; one shudders just to think of it.

OCTOBER 22D

Semi-official newspapers with wide circulations, such as the *Petit Parisien,* whose policy has consisted during the last twenty years in giving a roseate hue to the worst news so as not to alarm their readers, now publish lengthy panegyrics of Jacques Bainville [1] and his realistic views of Germany.

Never silent, Bainville foresaw certain catastrophes in Europe, and present events have, if possible, surpassed his prophecies. For as a pessimist once remarked: pessimists are wrong in one thing only and

[1] A famous historian and journalist, whose reputation has never stopped growing since his death. He edited the foreign politics column of the *Action Française* and was chief editor of the *Revue Universelle.*

that is in not being pessimistic enough. I saw Bainville at close quarters when I was his secretary at the
Revue Universelle. What struck me most was the
extraordinary solitude which encompassed this man
in spite of the incense wafted to him daily by hundreds of thousands of readers. He was haughty and
dry, in the eyes of superficial observers, because he
was modest, but he suffered silently from the stupidity of the human race, as one suffers for an in-
valid relative. (He hinted at the secret movements of
his sensibilities in a strange book, *Jaco et Lori*.) I remember one day he was brought an evening paper,
the headlines of which announced one or another of
Germany's innumerable violent and capricious decisions; Bainville drummed on his desk with one
hand, murmuring two lines of doggerel which he
would often quote with a bitter irony:

Ce serait une erreur de croire que ces choses
Finiront par des chants et des apothéoses.[1]

Another time, Bainville was asked to speak at a
big public meeting about France's foreign policy; he
impulsively made a gesture of repugnance: "Talk in
public! Oh, no! I could never play up to the public
like a low comedian. . . ."

He literally lived "by his stove," like Descartes,
and I can see him now, sitting one winter's day at his
desk in the Rue du Bac, all but leaning against a stove,
which exhaled so much carbonic gas that the air was

[1] *It would be an error to think that these things*
Will end with songs and apotheoses.

suffocatingly close. Bainville noticed nothing, nor was he aware of the poisonous smell, being completely absorbed by the pages which he was finishing on the latest metamorphosis of Pan-Germanism, pages containing many prophetic truths. One day a traveller returning from Germany told him that Hitler's photograph could be seen everywhere there, in official or public buildings, in shops, in private houses. Bainville made a remark which sounded like a paradox: "It's in France that the Führer's portrait should be hung everywhere, to prevent the French from squabbling endlessly. . . . Yes, if I were master of this country, I would order the Nazi dictator's likeness to be placed everywhere. And perhaps at administration meetings, at parliamentary sessions, at union meetings and government councils, certain discussions could be avoided, because the bickerers would suddenly realize that *he* was looking at them, *he* was listening to them and even that *he* was smiling with satisfaction."

The posthumous glory of Bainville, developing in the most unexpected circles during the first months of this war is a curious sign. The sudden interest taken in the Danubian problems is another. It took the war to make many minds come out of their shells, if I may thus express myself, and make them think about Europe, for a Frenchman is usually so happy in his own home that he lives contentedly behind closed doors. Friedrich Sieburg noted this correctly. I remember that in 1937 the reason which he most often advanced to convince French people of the end of Austria's independence was this: "You

French will do nothing to defend Vienna because you aren't interested in Europe."

Other minds besides Bainville's predicted justly and exactly the evolution of Germany, and the truth about Nazism was not the monopoly of a single party. But at the time, they were stoned, or else ears were stopped so as not to hear these prophecies. What is most astonishing in Cassandra's case is that her name should have been handed down to posterity, for usually the crowd's first movement against bores and hindrances (or so it usually considers those who foresee too clearly) is to stifle them by a conspiracy of silence.

Arthur said to me the other day in his inimitable slang: "Well, we certainly put our fingers in our eyes about the *Fridolins*." (*Fridolins,* in World War Number Two, is the term most frequently used by soldiers to designate those whom World War Number One called *Boches*.)

And Arthur was right. It makes one dizzy to think of all the nonsense about Germany spoken and believed in all countries for the last twenty years; nonsense which I have swallowed along with everyone else, of course. . . . That the man in the street should give credit to such foolishness is natural enough, but that certain personages, high up in international politics, should also have seen things wrongly, when they should have had first hand information, transcends all imagination.

It is true enough that many of the reports sent from Berlin to the Quai d'Orsay and the Foreign Office by the French and British Embassies were not even read in Paris and London and were put to sleep among bundles of dust-covered papers in the archives. At least, that is what was told me at the French Embassy in Berlin.

There is something more mysterious still: it is that an unquestionably intelligent man can go completely astray concerning such and such a political problem, where a mediocre mind will see his way clearly. It must be that intelligence is so unsure, even among those who are richly provided with it, that it risks going back on them at any moment; even with those most gifted in intellect it seems to shine out intermittently. . . . Thus, Philippe Berthelot, a man most assuredly above the average, made the following remark to me when Hitler came into power: "Germany reminds me of certain dogs that howl when they are chained up and, that when off the lead yelp in a friendly fashion at your side. . . . Hitler is going to govern; that is, free the dog, and then all will be quiet and peaceful once more. . . ." Now that the events of several years later show that those who passed as the "princes of intellect" could be wrong to such an extent, one does not feel proud of the human brain. . . .

OCTOBER 23D

————•◦•————

An officer back from the Maginot Line told me that mysterious hands had brought to his sector the text of a song printed at Stuttgart: "Have you seen the Englishman?" Three days ago, Mr. Chamberlain announced to the Commons that certain elements of British troops had taken possession of their sector at the front. It is evident that the "English problem" is a most delicate psychological problem which the services of the High Commissariat of Information must solve as quickly as possible.

A letter that I received from London last week gave me to understand that the morale is good there, that people feel safely protected behind the French Army and that the British are preparing for a long war; wearing out Germany seems to be the idea.

At the same time, certain average Frenchmen think that all is for the best, with the British Fleet in control of the seas, and they also hope that the blockade will of itself alone bring Germany to her knees. But the blockade of 1939 is not that of 1914: Germany has access to all kinds of doors, and most important ones, which were closed to her twenty-five years ago. And it seems to me that the truth on this subject has been written by General Duval in one of his recent articles: that a war such as this one cannot be waged without decisive results obtained on terra firma battlefields.

When the French or the English, giving way to a very human inclination, both imagine that it is the other of them that will have most of the work to do, it means that whichever party thinks that way does not possess the necessary combative habit of mind. Arthur vindicates my opinion with proof: "Nothing to worry about," he says. "The English and all their boats prowling the seas and then . . . and then, *mon vieux,* they have Canada!" Evidently, Canada, for Arthur, represents a sort of Golconda and a good deal more besides. We are never sufficiently aware of the manner in which facts are deformed by the popular imagination, and a person with thorough knowledge of the concierge class psychology would certainly get up better propaganda texts than a university professor.

OCTOBER 24TH

It is announced once more that Hitler is holding a mysterious council of war which may perhaps decide the fate of all of us. And at the same time it is persistently whispered that several of the Hohenzollerns have been thrown into prison. . . .

Amid the mass of information printed in one country at war about another country at war, how few items ring true. Doubtless, for purposes of our cause, resistance to pure Hitlerism is exaggerated; and yet this resistance, be it mental, military or economic, certainly exists. Dictators have succeeded in imposing upon their foes a highly simplified image of themselves, and a highly advantageous one. We fall into the trap. We look at these gentlemen and see them, not as they are, but as they are shown by a legend which they have manufactured. At last we come to believe that they have only to speak to be obeyed, that by pressing a button they can provoke the end of the world, and we suppose them to be incapable of uncertainty. But after all, they are but men like ourselves, even if they are monsters in some respects, and they work with other men as ambitious and as unscrupulous as themselves; and some days this cannot be plain sailing. Mussolini has admitted that in the early days of Fascism he spent twelve hours out of the twenty-four in keeping on good terms with his friends; this left him three hours only in which to study problems of public welfare. (And this is perhaps why, in its beginnings, the Fascist regime made so few breaks.)

If democracies suffer from an evil called demagogy, this does not mean that dictatorships are free from formidable internal ills, and precisely that of demagogy. It is fair to surmise that the world will be astounded, some fifty years hence, when it is discovered how at certain moments the fate of a dictator's career trembled in the balance; just as we are surprised nowadays on reading the details of all the opposition and treason strewn along Napoleon's path.

OCTOBER 25TH

I have been reminded of what I wrote in this journal a few days ago about the errors in judgment by intelligent men, for a friend has just shown me the following fine sentences:

"The more danger in the world, the more must disarmament be achieved." (Léon Blum in 1932) Also this remark of Sir Arthur Balfour's regarding the Russian problem: "One of the greatest menaces to peace today is the totally unarmed condition of Germany."

OCTOBER 27TH

I learn that I have been assigned to the Ministry of Information, in the North American Department. So I shall leave the barracks and am no longer to hear Arthur's free appreciations of men and events; in other words I shall no longer be kept informed about the morale of my compatriots. . . .

NOVEMBER 2D

If someone had entered Saint-Germain-des-Prés at eleven o'clock a few days ago, without having been forewarned, that person would have been much surprised; he or she would have heard the tune of

"Deutschland über alles" resounding to the vaulted roof of this ancient church from the chapel back of the high altar. And this person would have seen French officers standing at attention while this anthem was played on the harmonium; and a solemn expression on the faces of these officers. A little while before the hymn was played a priest had spoken in German and many eyes were filled with tears. . . . And alone in his rank, on a chair placed ahead of the others, a young man had listened to the sermon; at the end of the ceremony he was the first to leave the nave and as he passed, the men bowed very low and the women curtsied. . . .

All around the chapel hung white and red flags; it was Saint Leopold's feast day and the Austrian colony in Paris, joined by some French, prayed fervently for the resurrection of Austria. Among others present was a woman whose son, a few days before, had barely escaped being interned in France as an "enemy subject." And then, fortunately, this boy who had left Vienna under dramatic circumstances after the *Anschluss* had been able to prove that he was an "enemy subject"—but also an enemy of the Nazis, and he was there, at Saint-Germain-des-Prés, in the little group that has promised to defend Prince Otto of Habsburg, if need be, at the expense of their lives.

Two pictures came to my mind during this singular Mass: the picture of Schuschnigg and that of Mussolini. Because Schuschnigg, in Vienna, spoke to me of his country in 1935, in a "hoping against all hope" fashion which was his alone. Less than a

year before, the Nazis had assassinated Dollfuss, and
Schuschnigg had kept on trying to save Austria by
every means in his power, against tide and weather.
The Chancellor had nothing of the tribune in his
aspect: of medium height, his gold-rimmed specta-
cles and extremely sober face made him resemble
one of the professors who can be seen, in any provincial Austrian town, taking a walk on Sundays
accompanied by their little families; and the students who pass them in the quiet streets salute them
stiffly and most respectfully. Schuschnigg had come
to the Ministry of Education, on the Minoritenplatz,
accompanied by a small guard of young Catholics in
uniform who wore an armband bearing a cross
which was not the swastika, and whose salute was
not the Hitlerian salute. In the drawing room where
I waited was a large portrait of the Empress Elizabeth and another of the Archduke Rodolph, and
each likeness of Austria's masters conjured up a
terrible tragedy. . . . The same morning, I had gone
to the Ballplatz and there the drawing room had
been shown where Dollfuss, streaming with blood,
had been laid upon a sofa (the little man had been
struck by his murderers' bullets as he was desperately attempting to open a locked door, and his
fingers had contracted on the doorknob as he was
shot in the back). A picture of the Virgin glowed
softly, illuminated by a watchlight, near the spot
where he who was called the martyr chancellor had
fallen. And in Schuschnigg's office, the death mask
of his unhappy predecessor was laid on the table.
There was drama everywhere, an unlucky spell

seemed to have been cast over the fine baroque rooms of the Ballplatz where the fate of a country . . . the fate of Europe . . . was to be decided. For from the day when the *Anschluss* took place, the game was lost, as was seen later. France and England who had promised on three solemn occasions, putting their signatures to parchment documents, to save the independence of Austria, did not budge; they did nothing, not even as much as their feeble show at saving . . . Ethiopia. (In Paris, at the time of the *Anschluss,* there was no government, for the cowardly deed was carried out during a political crisis.) And this time Italy did not move. She was now in the German camp, she who in July, 1937 had mobilized on the Brenner and in part prevented the annexation of Austria by Germany from occurring that year instead of later.

Between the first attempt at annexation in 1934 and the second, a sojourn in Rome took me to the Palazzo Venezia to see Signor Mussolini. Returning from Austria, I came there to ask certain questions of the dictator and was surprised to find that I aroused the ex-journalist within him; for, according to tactics well-known in our profession, he transformed the questioner into the one who is questioned. The conversation turned chiefly on Austrian affairs. And this in spite of the fact that at that time (it was May, 1935) other topics held much attention and Abyssinia was already being greatly discussed, as it was to be attacked in the autumn.

Signor Mussolini still received journalists in 1935 and he seemed to them to be very different from his legendary self, very different from the Duce who gesticulates on a balcony and whom we have all seen so often in the newsreel. He used to speak to his visitors in a very gentle voice, without ceasing to look at them with an intensity which varied according to the subject of conversation; and he also practised in a masterly fashion an art which all the great of this world usually lack: the art of listening. He had certainly seen hundreds of informers far better qualified than I, and they had surely long since told him the essentials concerning Austria; and yet the head of the Italian Government still wished to know this, or that, returning to questions of detail, and particularly wanting to find out what impression the leaders of the country made upon the average Austrian living in cities or on the land. ("Is President Miklas *a reality* to them?" Or else: "What do the provinces think of Starhemberg?" etc. . . .) The role of individuals in politics clearly appeared to him as a determining factor and it was natural that his personal experience of this should have rooted the idea in his mind. He told me that he would give me his opinion on the essentials of the Austrian problem as it appeared at the time. I feared that his declarations would be both extremely vague and excessively prudent, but, on the contrary, when the time came he expressed himself in a far more categorical fashion than I could have hoped:

"Austria as she now is cannot live, and it certainly is not the League of Nations which will save her. The government in power is full of good intentions, but it does not possess the emphatic voice suited to present circumstances, the revolutionary voice. There is but one solution," he added, "yes, one thing alone could save the country: the return of the Habsburgs."

Signor Mussolini developed this point of view at length; which might surprise his hearer, for the Italy of May, 1935 was beginning to form rather close connections with Nazi Germany and the Third Reich's sentiments toward the Habsburgs were well-known. True, I have often asked myself whether the words which I heard were sincere: yet there was no reason why the head of the Italian Government should take the trouble to mystify a visitor who had promised (this was one of the conditions of the meeting) not to publish anything in a French newspaper that had been told him. And when statesmen know that their conversation will not be repeated, they usually stop lying. And so I have reason to believe that these remarks as to the only solution which could have prevented the *Anschluss,* were the sincere opinion of the man who made them, seated in his enormous office, occasionally sipping some herb tea from a cup on his desk. . . .

And now that the *Anschluss* is accomplished, now that Italy has made a pact with the Hitlerian devil and the European war is upon us, this little scene has returned to my memory; and as I looked at Archduke Otto during that strange Mass this morning, I could not help thinking of all that might have been, of all that might have prevented things from coming to this present pass, in Austria and also in France— and in Italy.

NOVEMBER 3D

Will this war of Sioux and trappers and advanced outposts long continue? For this is really Indian warfare, with all its ruses and, for good measure, the "pleasing embellishment" of modern weapons. Captain Berthier, who has just returned from "out there," told me that he and a few privates went into a house abandoned the other day by Germans. That is to say, these men spent hours in uncovering the innumerable pitfalls which await visitors in these habitations, traps which at last are becoming known. For instance, you lay a hand on the front-door knob and that determines the explosion of a mine. After which, you enter and you notice at the far end of the room, over the mantelpiece, a portrait of the Führer: do not give way to an ill-tempered impulse and tear Hitler's picture from the wall, for that would immediately cause another explosion. There are also ten-franc pieces lying on the ground, apparently forgotten by someone; but as you bend to pick them up, you tread on a spring which may provoke a violent outburst. And when you throw away a dead hen "forgotten" on a bench, a string attached to one of its legs is found connected to an infernal machine. To think that at this time the greatest armies in the world spend their time on such childish tricks, un-

worthy of bad little schoolboys. . . . The variety of
these snares is limited, but each one is repeated with
nicety and on a wholesale scale.

Those who take part in reconnoitering expeditions
at night wear black, oiled clothes to escape the
enemy's clutch, and they are accompanied by dogs
specially trained for this kind of exploit. . . . Here
are other German ruses: to spring a rattle under a
blanket, which gives a good imitation of the noise
made by a machine gun and leads our watchers to
fire, thus revealing their positions. . . . Or else to
place bright lights at the end of long poles and then
wave them before our sentries so that they will show
themselves. . . .

In true German fashion, an imposing number of
malevolent hens and death-bearing portraits are
strewn over premises per square mile. But once the
trap has made a few victims, the entire sector is on
the alert. . . .

Another procedure, applied wholesale by another
gang of specialized Nazis is an entirely novel propaganda scheme: the letter trick. Soldiers receive letters
from the interior of France signed "a friend who
wishes your good," or sometimes even signed with
the name of someone they know. The soldiers are
informed that privations are growing numerous,
that their children will have no milk this winter,
that their wives are unfaithful to them with British non-commissioned officers (naturally, an Englishman is chosen, to make the blow more cruel), that
these officers receive a hundred francs as daily pay
and live comfortably in the best hotels, far from

the front. Other letters are sent in the opposite direction: that is, they are mailed from the army zone to strike at those who live behind it, and announce that epidemics have broken out in the Maginot Line, that the soldiers refuse to fight and that, anyway, the Germans refuse to attack the French, so there is but one thing to do and that immediately: to make peace with Hitler. Sometimes the text of the letters coincides word for word with the text of certain German radio broadcasts to the French.

There are also wild tales which do not hold water and which, quite by chance, are circulated here and there at the same moment. There is the story about the French aviator, who, with his companion, is obliged to make a forced landing in enemy territory. The plane is shattered as it grounds and, so the story runs, one of the pilots is killed. The Germans give the victim a magnificent funeral with *Marseillaise,* military honors, etc. . . . There is a speech before the coffin covered with the tricolor and the orator swears that the Nazis have no grudge against France. When the survivor expects to be put in prison, he is set free (!) and is once more assured that he can go back to his country because Germany has nothing against France, etc. . . . Those who repeat this anecdote guarantee its authenticity, for the sake of appearing well-informed, although they own to having heard the story from an indirect source.

This sort of story is often heard over the German radio and for this reason, the sending of radio sets to our regiments has been stopped. It was decided at first to make our men a present of these radios in order to help kill the long hours of waiting which is their daily lot. But it was noticed that the soldiers "caught" the German broadcasts, to "amuse" themselves (yet, while laughing over these broadcasts they could not help thinking them over later) and also because the broadcasts from the French posts did not "amuse" them at all.

I have been astounded to discover that the High Commissariat of Information does not possess Weapon Number One of modern information, the radio. For the State Radio, after long tribulation, is either the business of protégés who have been placed there for obscure motives of services rendered, or the prerogative of several ministries who are continually wrangling over it.

What remains for the unhappy head of French Propaganda? The press? Censorship steps between them and this does not exactly facilitate harmony between them. Photography? It can no longer accomplish anything. . . . As to the cinema, that has been almost completely disrupted by mobilization. . . .

For our mobilization did not foresee the designation of specialists to propaganda work, and for a good reason: propaganda, in our country, existed neither for civilians nor for ministries. It was only in August, 1939 that a Commissariat of Propaganda was timidly created; in September, 1939 it still was practically in embryo.

In other words, Germany has been waging *psy-*

chological war on us since 1933; in this war she disposes a well-drilled army, numerous weapons and munitions, powerful and perfected methods, trained leaders: to which we have nothing whatever to oppose. This is a one-way war.

Why? For a thousand reasons, but principally for one profound, far-reaching reason: on their side, there was but one thought, war. But in a country as civilized as ours there are plenty of other things to occupy our minds. With them, all energies are at the service of the State and its vast purposes. A monstrous monopoly with formidable results. With us, on the contrary, the State employs only those energies which have not found their application elsewhere.

Between France and Hitler's Germany today lies all the difference which distinguishes two living beings belonging to periods of biological evolution far removed from each other. Here, an animal whose functions and whose strength are turned solely to battle. There, a being whose functions are infinitely more varied and which are, in part, we might say, functions *de luxe,* using the term to mean magnificent superfluousness. This latter creature has scarcely any pinchers and no longer possesses anything but a carapace to ensure its security. . . .

What shows the extent of Hitler's plan is the fact that a military nation like Germany should not have confined herself this time to military methods but has understood the importance of a preliminary attack against the adversary's morale. The activities of Nazi propaganda since September 3, 1939 have merely continued the work begun after 1933. So the termites have been in the beams of our roofs for seven years: the enemy supposes rightly that a house whose roof caves in resists far less well than another when it is stormed.

NOVEMBER 4TH

An American journalist asked me whether or not I believed in a war of action: this is Question Number One. Great Heavens, how would I know? That is precisely what everyone of us is constantly wondering without being able to form a final opinion. Anyway, the more one reasons in certain cases, the less clearly one sees. . . . While, if one heeds a few intuitions, hesitation ceases. The one presentiment which I feel very strongly at present is that this spurious war cannot last very long. . . .

I sent my journalist—for he was eager for military certitudes—to the general who writes the bulletin for *Le Temps*. This general, speaking of the tactics employed by the German Army in Poland, concluded with these words: "Here, on the strategic level, we observe the use of grouped armored units corresponding to a determined theory which must have been the object of frequent peace-time exercises on the part of our enemy. We can suppose that such maneuvres will be repeated in the future. . . ."

NOVEMBER 8TH

The Commissariat of Information has been aware since yesterday that Belgium and Holland have attempted to mediate for peace. The news of this tentative proposal has not made much of an impression on the public, in spite of the fact that a great part of them do not believe in the genuineness of the war. At the same time, perhaps this portion of the public think that at present one is no longer "capable" of peace. In this world, how many continents or countries remain which are still "capable" of peace . . . ?

Now that I work at the Commissariat of Information I understand that this war has deprived the United States of many things which came from Europe, and, in particular, of news. No sooner was war declared than the belligerents either allowed very little information to filter through to foreign countries or they exported an incredible quantity of printed matter and photographs—the latter exports having a markedly biassed tendency. In the second category Germany distinguishes herself and sets forth on a real dumping propaganda in neutral countries. On the other hand, France forms a blockade around her own news and even to her own friends very quickly becomes an abstraction or an enigma.

The result of all this is that the American foreign

correspondent, no matter where his work may have
taken him in Europe since September, 1939, has not
had an easy time. He is obliged more or less to turn
himself into a smuggler.

The public, calmly reading its paper in New York
or switching on the radio, has no idea of the price
paid for the news which it receives; and that is true
of the most insignificant bits of information. I am
able to measure every day the tenacity and ingen-
iousness of American journalists. For reasons entirely devoid of malice, obstacles spring up and multiply under their feet; but nothing rebuffs them. In
my capacity as ex-journalist I sympathize with their
troubles, while I secretly note with admiration that
through sheer professional tenacity they prove themselves far superior to correspondents from all other
neutral countries. No one is more obstinate than
an American newspaperman attempting to obtain
news in a country at war which does not wish to
communicate anything about the country or the
war. And I begin to realize that in the heart of every
American man and woman slumbers a journalist:
"news" is a word which quickens the pulse.

At the Commissariat of Information, it is forbidden to give neutral journalists the texts of German communiqués, or, in a general way, the contents of dispatches from the Havas News Agency—
known as "forbidden sheets." Well, by a cleverly put
question or a mere allusion, such and such an American journalist lets it be understood that he has some
knowledge of the prohibited copy. . . . These journalists find some way of rounding the difficulty and

I can only suppose to myself that in their place I would have done the same.

Added to this, they are nothing if not plucky. One of them, in spite of the strictest orders, has succeeded in mingling with a corps of free lances during one of his visits to the front and in taking part in one of the "nocturnal promenades" of the said free lance corps. Another journalist has attempted for weeks to fly over Germany in a French reconnaissance plane and though he was obliged to relinquish the plan, it was not from lack of trying. Lastly, others spoke from French radio stations, presenting their fees to various charitable organisations.

All day long, newspaper correspondents come to see me, putting a thousand questions which the ex-bandit-journalist that I am finds most interesting, but which the functionary-gendarme I have become regards as extremely embarrassing.

During the night some representatives of the big radio networks ring me up. And how is one not to answer a broadcaster who wakes you up at two in the morning? Roused with a start, drowsy and dulled with sleep, during the first moments I find myself defenceless before my terrible questioners. Later, when I realize what I have said, I am terrified, but reassure myself with the thought that the censor follows in my wake: I can go back to bed in peace.

NOVEMBER 10TH

News of the attempt on the Munich Bierhalle had just come when a letter found on a German prisoner was shown me. It was a letter written to the soldier by his father, a peasant: "How much to be pitied are those who each day have to give up more of their beer and the fruit of their labor! Let's hope that we will be preserved from this. We still get bread and potatoes but we have ration cards for all other foods. . . ." The youth to whom these prosaic lines were addressed, is what is called a "hero." To all questions of a military order put by French officers, he replied by repeating: "Heil Hitler!" At first this may sound admirable but on thinking it over one cannot help feeling that the father's sentiments are nearer the truth than those of the young visionary.

Yes, the father talks of bread and potatoes and his Nazi compatriots doubtless judge him to be very material and most lukewarm towards the regime. For all that, what permits the continuity of civilization is rural stability, the attachment of the peasant to the soil, to the fruits of the earth, to his work and the goods resulting from work, as the author of this letter testifies. With Germans such as this, French peasants could get along; each one could for the common good carefully give this, to receive that. A Franco-

German dialogue between good peasants is reassuring for peace and fortunate for both peoples. While in abandoning these "terre-à-terre" values for "heroic" values one enters into an immense and sanguinary imposture. . . .

Here is another example of imposture: putting religion into politics. Witness the following text, published some time since by the S.S. review, *Das Schwarze Korps:* "On this day, I draw near to your image. This image is supernaturally large, limitless, formidable. It is hard, magnificent and sublime, it is simple, benevolent and warm. It is in one person our father, our mother and our brother, it is more still. . . . Thus you stand in the basilica of the love of millions of beings, a basilica whose luminous cupola rises to heaven, etc. . . ." And there is a lot more along the same lines, for this prayer to Hitler is by no means short.

If the French put no "love" at all into politics, the Nazis give a little too lavishly of theirs in that direction. . . .

NOVEMBER 12TH

In his speech on Armistice Day, the High Commissioner of Information spoke of the future armistice, touching lightly upon a great idea, namely, that the future must be conjured up to make the present acceptable. But what future? It cannot be described in all its details; one can be certain of one thing alone: that it will be, no matter what form it assumes, very different from the past.

Those who are fighting in the hope that life will begin again as it was before, with its good sides (leisure, liberties of all sorts, primacy of culture) and its more contestable aspects (selfishness of many wealthy persons, hostility to work in certain workmen, lack of national unity and brotherhood, frivolity in leaders, the absurdity of fine ladies who go to the Chamber of Deputies sessions as they would attend the Opera, etc. . . .) will be profoundly disappointed. The only difference is that if we are defeated, everything will be swept away, whereas if we are victorious, we will be able to keep *a few* of the aspects of our past life, but a few only. Great changes of every sort are inevitable; this is regrettable, in some respects heart-rending, but grieving will do no good, it is useless. Had we decided to remain neutral in order to escape these upheavals, such upheavals would have occurred just the same. . . . By closing one's door, one does not avoid feeling the shock of an earthquake. The Nazis have invented a means of making the earth quake, in every sense of the word, and things had best be looked in the face, just as they appear. As far as changes are concerned, up to the present they have only achieved destruction, but a day will come when reconstruction must be considered; and we must look upon that day with confidence.

For the time being, two things must remain ever-present in our memory:

1. We must win this war.

2. To a certain extent, revolution has followed the outbreak of this war. For modern wars are revolutions.

It is perhaps from fear of these landslides, these seismic shocks which are the inevitable consequences of any conflict, that so many people continue, even at the present moment, to close their eyes and behave as though the war did not exist. We cling desperately to our mode of life, while knowing at the bottom of our souls that this form of existence cannot last much longer. But we turn our heads away and cry out to destiny: "Just one moment more of happiness." This is a little cowardly, but most human.

Had lunch this morning with my brother who had returned from "somewhere in France," at the Restaurant du Rond-Point des Champs-Elysées. Around us what is called a most "Parisian" crowd where "Joans of Arc" dressed by Schiaparelli were not lacking, nor the few snobs who still take the Duke of Windsor for a true friend of the people and Herr von Ribbentrop for the cream of old German aristocracy. Met Hélène de Portes, as usual in a state of agitation: "Have you seen this morning's papers? Perfectly revolting. . . . The press is not properly directed, etc. . . ." She thinks that Daladier does not "galvanize" the papers, that the public morale feels the effect of this, and she added: "I know what I'm talking about, for I go through the papers every morning." It seems that she goes to the Ministry of Finances from time to time and looks at the newspapers in an office. . . . But it is not true, R. told me yesterday, that Reynaud sees only through her eyes. Often, too often, he follows her advice, but sometimes he lets a stream of words flow from his "counsellor's" lips without paying any attention to it. But it is a great pity that she courts public notice, for this leads a great many journalists to think that her case is the rule in all of our ministries, whereas, to my knowledge, no one has ever meddled so ostensibly as she with public affairs. . . .

As lunch ended, my brother said to me: "I prefer the air we breathe *out there* to what one breathes here. I will go back tomorrow without regret."

However, it would be a mistake to take this "Parisian" restaurant for Paris. At this very moment thousands and thousands of women are working in factories, and in the country are looking after deserted farms. They all bravely face their tasks, after having experienced an instant's surprise, for they had come to think for years that the most terrible of all days, the day of general mobilization, would never return.

And to these women it had been repeated *ad nauseam* that it would not be necessary to renounce traditional liberties and the many advantages which had been theirs. It is certain that this heritage of spiritual and material privileges handed down by a happy period would have been more easily retained by deciding *sooner* to give up a small part of it. Without doubt the war could have been avoided if, at the beginning of the menace, necessary sacrifices had been made; then the French State would have been stronger and better armed, so as to intimidate the Nazi adventurers in time. But the menace was taken lightly, we tried to minimize it—*and happiness puts people to sleep*. Not that all Frenchmen were happy, but they carried the art of living further than other people, possessed greater facilities than those in neighboring countries and did not know it. . . . The proof is to be found once more in a remark candidly made by Paul Reynaud in his last speech: "The rich continue to bring their money back to France. . . . The poor place their money at the country's disposal by increasing the savings which they put into banks." The involuntary humor of this sentence, where the "poor" are defined as those who have savings, was brought to my notice by a correspondent of the *Wall Street Journal*.

Well, Rich and Poor (with or without savings) for years have required a good deal of pressure in the matter of changing their mode of living. Everything goes on as if they thought that this mode of living could be kept up perpetually, as though comfort were the one thing in this world which could not change. . . . This age of butter does not wish to die, and butter, symbolic butter, has remained on all tables, in the same quantities as before, even when everyone realizes that cannons must be turned out night and day.

Butter reigned supreme at the "Rond-Point" this morning, as in normal times; and what is more, everyone seemed to know some way of getting around restrictions, no matter what. "Today, the serving of liqueurs is forbidden," the head waiter murmured under his breath; he added with a wink: "But if you want some *fine* ask the waiter for a cup of 'health tisane.'" As he bent over us to impart this great secret, I could see, pinned to the wall above his head, a poster announcing a new play called: *C'était histoire de rire.* ("It was Just for the Fun of the Thing.")

The idea that has prevailed for several years has evidently been that we could bear the supplementary load of rearmament without being condemned at the same time to very sharp privations. "France and her empire are so rich," our deputies would repeat, "that we will not have to suffer." Yet, simply from hearing this refrain in the mouths of people who wished to be re-elected, we should have had our doubts. . . . I have my doubts, particularly since the war—since the unforeseen form taken by this spurious war; a constant effort must be made not to believe that we are living in peace time. "Business as usual. . . ." This time-worn device is the slogan of the moment, and Paul Reynaud again the other day enlarged upon the idea before a few of us. If new models are being turned out by the dressmakers, as though nothing in particular were happening, he said, this is an excellent thing, for the sale of these gowns will bring in currency with which we can buy machinery, tools, etc. . . . I quite agree, but there is also another most important factor in war time: the "climate" or atmosphere peculiar to a war, the atmosphere which gives reality to the country's efforts. According to whether the atmosphere exists or not, the morale is very different, and that is as important as the deposit of a certain number of foreign banknotes in our banks.

Let us be frank: we like the formula "Business as Usual" because it is owing to this we continue to put as much as possible of "peace in the war" while our enemy for the last six years has placed war in peace.

NOVEMBER 14TH

What do we principally see in this Hotel Continental, which shelters the services of the Commissariat of Information? Bedrooms, transformed into offices; and each bedroom has a bathroom and—a professor. There are 400 collaborators in this ministry and they are divided up thus:

Professors 65%
Retired diplomats 20%
Miscellaneous professions 13%
Journalists 2%

A great many of these masters have names that are respected, and their merit, as indeed their fame, is not to be doubted. But are they the right men in the right place?

It has been said, it has even been written, that our Republic was a Republic of professors, and I am beginning to understand what was meant by this. And what is more, I would have perceived this at once had I meditated over the dazzling career of the deputy from my quarter, the Honorable Tartempion.

Mr. Tartempion is purely a politician, the hundred percent political article. Once I went to one of his electoral meetings and I admired his ability to please just by showing his fat, jolly face, his skill in not answering questions, the frightfully platitudinous turn of his eloquence and the valor with which he clinks glasses with elector after elector, at the *bistrot,* after the speeches. Tartempion is one of those whose watchword is the celebrated exclamation: "Always to the left, but no further!" In principle he has some advanced ideas, but in the lobbies of the Chamber he wages campaigns against too audacious reforms. At bottom he is the worst type of reactionary, the revolutionary who talks constantly of going forward and does not budge. But when he lingers a little too long on what he himself calls the "terrain of ideas," Tartempion becomes extremely uneasy; his brow streams with perspiration, his sufferings are as keen as when he quotes a word of Greek origin—technocracy, for instance (his tongue trips and the syllables come tumbling out in unorthodox order). Though Tartempion rarely gives way to ambitious flights of oratory, he tells his secretary in confidence that it is necessary to slip "some highbrow subject" into a speech from time to time, in order to create a serious atmosphere. For Tartempion has a secretary and when Tartempion became minister (this has happened to him four times), his secretary, who happens to be one of my schoolboy friends and as such does not conceal from me such pearls as drop from his master's lips, was made head of a department. And whom had Tartempion chosen for his secretary? An assistant professor from the University of Paris.

For a politician, particularly when he is minister, feels the need of protection against his own incompetence, to say nothing of masking it from the eyes of others. With a Normal School graduate by his side he feels quite secure. His Excellency Tartempion's choice has been repeated thousands of times (literally, for there are over a thousand ex-ministers living in our Republic): ministers invariably attract the University, using it as a garment, like the one thrown over Noah to conceal his nakedness.

When the Commissariat of Information was created, professors, from force of habit, invaded the place in serried ranks, preceded by Jean Giraudoux, an exquisite writer, himself a graduate of the Ecole Normale—like a bird of paradise being hatched in an incubator. As the Ministry of Foreign Affairs also had a word to say about the organisation of the Commissariat, it deputed a small army of ambassadors and ex-ministers recalled to active service to fit the circumstances. But what exactly was it all about?

Information and propaganda. Well, it would be a mistake to think that any Tom, Dick or Harry could be good at this kind of work and that anyone, by taking a pen to paper, is qualified for such a job.

Not that propaganda should be placed on a pedestal; on the contrary, it must be deplored that it has been given the rank which it occupies today and that it should hold such a considerable position in modern life. This is another thing which we owe to Nazi Germany. For years the Secret Weapon invented in the Third Reich's laboratories has been discussed; anything could be expected, even bacteriological warfare, but we never realized that the weapon had been in use against us for a long time, and that it was highly camouflaged and super-efficient propaganda.

Now that the poison has been put in circulation throughout the whole world, it is necessary that a counterpoison be used; this is quite evident. It is also deplorable, but the fact remains that propaganda has become as unpleasantly inevitable as the din of klaxons in the streets or the publicity proclaiming the excellence of X's Tomato Juice or Y's Cigarettes, announcements which are now always sandwiched in between a symphony by Mozart and one of Beethoven's quartets on the radio. . . . We cannot stop our ears and refuse to answer the Hitlerian offensive. In short, we cannot permit totalitarian "ideas" little by little to take possession of the brains, and particularly of the youthful brains, of the future and in all parts of the world. Thus the democracies find themselves obliged, sooner or later, to create a propaganda for democracy, and this is repugnant to them and seems to them anti-democratic. And that is why they act late rather than early and more often not at all.

In France it was decided very late, only a few days before war was declared, to create a tiny little General Commissariat of Information, and when war did break out, this modern organization had scarcely emerged from chaos. As soon as it came into being it rapidly took on an academic turn.[1]

Perhaps if Prof. Einstein were asked to drive a truck, he would do it very badly. Certainly he would know more about mechanics than any chauffeur but he probably would not possess reflexes worthy of the worst driver.

Fortunately for the professor, one thing is not measured and doled out to him or, in a general way, to the scholar, and that thing is time. A master of English letters is not obliged to decide before one-thirty (the hour when evening editions go to press) whether Shakespeare was really Shakespeare or whether he was the Earl of Derby. . . . But the propagandist, most especially, must find before one-thirty the theme of the hour or the refutation of the latest German fable; if he knows his business properly he must not only counterattack but even take the offensive.

There is a category of men who are trained by their profession to describe a scene and to draw from this scene conclusions, all in a minimum of time; and to describe what they have seen in a form that

[1] Gertrude Stein in *Paris France* gives the following explanation of the failure of the French propaganda: "Propaganda is not French, it is not civilized to want other people to believe what you believe because the essence of being civilized is to possess yourself as you are, and if you possess yourself as you are you of course cannot possess any one else, it is not your business."

will arrest the attention of the public. In truth, they
are the public's delegate (or its slave) and they are
also the slaves of their watches: a double servitude.
To sum up the Coronation of the King of England
by telephone and to make others see it in a quarter
of an hour as one has during five long hours; to
choose the details and those only which will interest
the masses; to relate before the microphone the
session at the House of Commons where Mr. Chamberlain announced his departure for Munich . . .
etc. Skilled accomplishments which the celebrities
of education and literature can perform very rarely.
For in the intellectual order, it is not always true
that he who is capable of doing more can necessarily
be capable of doing less.

And so it is, that in giving way to habits of minute
examination, in putting dots on mental I's, in sur-
rendering to the taste for delicate shading which
characterizes really refined minds, our professors at
the Commissariat of Information publish after considerable delay a species of literature destined only
for the élite. And this when speed and widespread
diffusion are the chief conditions for efficient information and propaganda. Ten lines of refutation
at the right time would be better than an exhaustive
and inexpedient report released at the end of the
month.

Also, it is not so important to furnish analyses and
diagnoses as it is to find remedies, no matter how
simple. Little by little, at the Hotel Continental,[1]
we are getting to *know* perfectly well what is not

[1] The seat of the Commissariat of Information.

working in favor of France in such and such a country, but our actions are insignificant compared with our knowledge.

Devotion and good will are everywhere very great and many of our collaborators are exhausted by their work. Some days, Giraudoux looks very badly. Yesterday I was also struck by the weary aspect of another writer who works in our ministry.

"Ten hours a day in my office here and, besides, I must prepare radio broadcasts," he confided to me.

"What are you going to tell your listeners?"

"I'm doing 'Colors during the war.'"

Seeing my surprise, he explained that he was about to begin a series of "variations" on blue, red, green, yellow etc.

These peculiar whimsicalities and the general lack of efficiency are irritating and at the same time disarming. France is all the more touching when she forms ideas of Chinese-like subtlety on such and such a subject—charming and elaborate ideas. And it is so like her to have chosen an author who is intelligible only to the happy few to talk to the great public, to have opposed the "Ariel" of our literature to Dr. Goebbels, a lame devil who prepares poisoned pills only too well.

NOVEMBER 15TH

"In these memorable battles," says a great historian, "our soldiers had the feeling that a prodigious rearguard, formed by the whole nation, stood behind them in support." And he thus describes the decrees issued by the French Revolution: "All the French are permanently commandeered. . . . The young men will fight; married men will forge weapons and transport sustenance. Women will make tents and clothes and serve in hospitals; children will make lint; old men, in public places, will encourage the warriors, teaching hatred of kings and the unity of the republic. . . ." [1] It is clear that during the French Revolution, Dynamics and Democracy were not separated. . . .

NOVEMBER 16TH

Yesterday we were told confidentially that the Germans, a very short while ago, had been on the point of invading Belgium, and that it is most sur-

[1] *Histoire de la Révolution Française,* Michelet.

prising that the thing did not take place between the 11th and 14th of this month. It is said that secret deliberations between the King of the Belgians and the Queen of Holland made the Nazis think twice, but this was no adequate explanation. At this writing, the German disposition of attack still is in position. The High Command has asked us to develop the following theme, in reply to comments instigated by this menace against the Low Countries: "The principal line of fortifications surrounding the Fortress of France today runs uninterruptedly to the North Sea. On the other hand, Belgium, with her fortified frontier and her considerably reinforced army can no longer be considered a negligible adversary. However, thanks to very great superiority in the men and material which they are able to concentrate against this little country, the Germans could hope to break through the fortified Belgian line rather rapidly and launch their armored forces in the direction of Brussels. The first advantages resulting from this type of attack would bring about reactions which cannot be foreseen at the present moment; but these advantages might, in the mind of the enemy command, be the occasion for initial successes, after which a breach in the fortified line of the North might be attempted. A major offensive through Belgium and also through southern Dutch territory appears to be the best solution for the Germans.

"But from a tactical point of view these successes would be much more difficult to realize. Strategically, this maneuver would encounter conditions far less favorable, because a complete surprise is impossible to obtain and because the mass of the German right wing would find its way blocked by the powerful Franco-British reserves."

The High Command, in declaring that the fortifications continue to the sea, puts an end to the debate which had begun in the Chamber in February, 1937. At the beginning of that year, a deputy (Monsieur de Chappedelaine) had put forward an enquiry on this theme: "And the North?" And other deputies had asked the same question. Monsieur Daladier replied: "Our system of fortifications, which I am prolonging, *although I have encountered opposition from various quarters,* along the northern frontier to Dunkerque. . . ." On December 3d of the same year, he spoke more clearly of this "opposition": "On the frontier in the North, *in spite of the advice of a very great number of high military authorities, who for years and years have declared that the fortification of the North was impossible to realize,* works have been built under satisfactory conditions. The work is proceeding. We must not forget that the fortifications must always be adapted at the same time to the nature of the soil, the lay of the terrain and the topography of the country. Naturally, we cannot think of building in Flanders fortifications of the type erected on the frontiers of Alsace and of Lorraine. . . ."[1]

[1] The *Journal Officiel* for 1937, which I re-read in New York and found most instructive, notes that a certain Parmentier, deputy from the North, made the following remark during this session: "Belgium in her northern and western regions, apart from the Ardennes, offers no difficulty of passage." Monsieur Daladier interrupted the orator then to say: "Do you think so?"

NOVEMBER 18TH

Conformity in the army is naturally more frequently found among old leaders, and when they remain a long time in office these leaders constitute a terrible danger: the world changes, the conditions of war, like those of peace, change, but the system of conformists does not change. This peril has existed at all times, and even before 1914 the "old fellows" smiled as they listened to the "young fellows," as though the latter's ideas were taken from one of Jules Verne's novels; Captain Berthier explained this to me yesterday.

It seems that the leaders who from 1914 to 1918 revealed the most surprising capacities had up to that time shown independent, almost heretical minds. Thus, the obscure colonel who before 1914 had repeated that war could no longer be waged without considerable materiel, and that bayonet attacks could no longer prevail against the "fire that kills," had been looked at askance by his superiors: the precursor of the period was to become Marshal Pétain. In those times, a representative of the General Staff (this was in 1909), declared: "Gentlemen, you talk to us of heavy artillery. Thank God, we have none." The head of the infantry affirmed, in 1910, that the use of the machine gun would change nothing in the art of war, and the Commander of the War School, after attending an aviation meeting, concluded that "this was sport, and for the army it meant nothing at all, zero." Result: in 1914, there were three hundred heavy French cannons against eleven hundred German cannons, two thousand machine guns against five thousand, and one hundred and sixty planes against two hundred and thirty. Conformity had already made ravages before 1914; and it made even greater ones when the "young fellows" of before 1914, wearing the halo of the 1918 victory, continued in office as late as 1939.

The "law of least imagination" has stopped new ideas on the threshold of General Headquarters; the latter has, little by little, imposed the dogma of its infallibility, and this law has ruled military policy, just as the law of least effort has governed plain politics. Berthier asserted with great heat that memory had spoken louder than imagination and so, by habit of long standing, preparations for the War of 1914 have been under way ever since 1919. The Maginot Line, that enormous extension of the 1914 trenches, would rise up like a sort of protest of the old war against the new one, capable at once of annihilating the invader and . . . the bold military theories of the new school. Captain Berthier is also indignant that only the defensive spirit of France has been exalted. It seems that a general wrote in the *Mercure de France,* in 1936, in the following terms: "France, peaceful and on the defensive, can only be against motorization." General Maurin, Minister of War, had already declared on June 3,

1935, in the Chamber: "How can anyone suppose that we still think in terms of an offensive when we have spent billions in establishing a fortified barrier? Could we be mad enough to go beyond this barrier seeking Heaven knows what adventure?" In other words, a war would have become just a species of fire insurance for many leaders who have forgotten the very meaning of a war—and who have demonstrated it with their *a priori* admission, for years, that war would take place in *our country* and not in theirs. It is true that every opportunity was taken to celebrate in lyrical terms the "shield" of France, the Maginot Line, and that the creation of the "sword" was refused in 1935—by the sword I mean the ten shock divisions demanded at that period by Reynaud. . . . As though a combatant could ever fell his adversary with no sword but only a shield.

I believe Berthier's views are extreme and his conclusions too black, but I concede that the military policy of France is incompatible with a foreign policy which has saddled her with responsibilities and has implicitly turned the army into Gendarme Number One of the League of Nations. When the first crime is committed at such and such a point in Europe, will the gendarme go and restore order? Or will he find that he is not prepared for punitive expeditions, and content himself with remaining in his armored sentry box, in front of his own house? This has been the problem at every diplomatic crisis in recent years. . . . We have not made up our minds to create an instrument to back up the foreign policy that has been chosen, but have continued to protest that we would remain, as in the past, faithful to the mutual assistance idea. Monsieur Léon Blum, then prime minister, repudiated in the first months of 1937 the theory of perpetual defensive and gave assurances that France would not remain an indifferent spectator. Monsieur Daladier, Minister of War, stirred up unanimous applause by swearing that "France will not remain motionless on her ramparts while a conflagration rages in Europe . . . etc."

In short, all was perfect on paper and the circle had been squared. . . . It remains to be found why those who lied always kept the good will of electors, to the detriment of those who spoke the truth. Because they showed life in roseate colors, as I said to Captain Berthier.

Yes, but also because democracies change their ideas very slowly, and mostly under the punitive action of events. "Look," he added. "See what has happened in England. . . . It is said that the English are blind, and this is true, but a certain number of them have not lacked courage when the occasion arose. A politician like Baldwin himself declared in 1937 that, as far as war in the air was concerned, the only defensive was the offensive and that bombers would always get by any line of anti-aircraft defence."

Yes, and later on in the famous speech [1] where he told how he had resolved to hide the truth from the country in order to secure favorable results in the elections, he pronounced a sentence which condemns

[1] November 12, 1936.

the vices of the democratic system more gravely than all of Hitler's insults: "A democracy is always two years behind the dictators."

NOVEMBER 24TH

Last night, gala evening at the Opera, for I can't remember what benevolent fund. Polish, English and French national anthems played to a rather incongruous audience, a good many nurses in uniform and the men in day clothes. It had been decided not to dress—the artificial state of peace in which we live not daring to live up to its appearances. Indeed, it would have been difficult to explain to the soldiers at the front that while they lived with their feet in the mud, other men put on white ties. . . . The spectators were more than a little bored, and then, the "festival" had an official character as the President of the Republic was present in a stage box, passing absent-mindedly as usual between lines of indifference.

In another stage box were the Duke and Duchess of Windsor, who had been invited by some friends who asked me to join the party. The "Festin de l'Araignée" was performed, in which the characters are insects. So the names of all these insects had to be translated, as well as one could, for the Duchess. It was like a class in English, and every one of us

pleaded ignorance in turn. After which the Duke
said that if he wished, he could do something for
the soldiers; that is, he could knit, for he had been
taught as a child to knit. "For a child," he remarked,
"can't always read, can he? So knitting is an excellent occupation." This was the second time that I
had been at a party where the ex-King of England
said whatever passed through his mind. (The last
time I had seen him was at an evening party in Paris
where he had hummed refrains in German.) During
the intermission a few of the ladies from the Red
Cross were presented to the Duchess and the usual
catastrophe occurred: some of the ladies made a
curtsy and others did not . . . an incident sufficient
to be the topic of conversation with certain people
for at least three days. . . . After which came a number of petty episodes and the smallest of small talk,
which Marcel Proust alone could have made interesting.

NOVEMBER 26TH

We have just been informed that Chancellor
Wirth, ex-German prime minister at the time of the
Weimar Republic, had declared that the Russo-
German Pact of August, 1939 was but the crowning
of a policy practised by official Germany, openly or
secretly, long before Hitlerism. Wirth owned that

the real aim of the Rapallo Pact in 1922 was to insure the military collaboration of Germany and Russia. This treaty allowed Germany to slip out of a
great number of the military clauses in the Treaty
of Versailles, and it was agreed that General von
Seeckt could proceed to carry out a few interesting
experiments in the U.S.S.R. (tank maneuvres, new
planes, etc. . . .) without being bothered by the inter-
Allied Control. On the other hand, this pact, now
seventeen years old, had as its ultimate and always
secret goal the assassination of Poland. "Good Doctor Wirth," as he was long called in France, even
tried to foment, through *agents provocateurs,* a Polish aggression which, had it taken place, would have
immediately drawn upon itself a crushing onslaught
from the conjoined Russian and German forces.
France would have been "appeased" by fine tirades
about peace, and England would probably not have
budged, or so it was thought—even then.

NOVEMBER 27TH

Fine tirades about peace? . . . It is true that they
have always made an enormous impression upon us
during the past few years precisely because as civilized men we indulge only one fanaticism, the fanaticism of peace. And I recall certain intonations in
voices, certain gestures, during a visit to the Hotel

Vierjahreszeiten, in Munich in 1938, at the end of that year.

A few weeks after the Munich agreement, *Paris-Soir* had sent me to find out what was being plotted in Germany and to interview Herr von Ribbentrop.

The Reich's Minister of Foreign Affairs occupied an apartment in the old Munich hotel, where Monsieur Daladier had spent a memorable night the month before. It seems that he did justice to the meals which were served him and did not disdain the Rhine wines. After dinner, Herr von Ribbentrop went to a corner of the hotel hall and sat there with a few of his collaborators to spend an evening in the way Germans love: an evening among intimates with beer and cigars. Apparently no measures had been taken for the protection of Herr von Ribbentrop, and anyone could have entered the hotel without difficulty; the powerful, luxurious Mercedes car decked with pennants which was stationed permanently before the door of the hotel testified clearly enough that an important man lived there. Accompanied by an interpreter in S.S. uniform, Herr von Ribbentrop spoke to me first in German and then, not without difficulty, in English and in French. The boldest questions were often received best; a few remarks I made to him regarding the prospect of disarmament, which might be considered after the Munich agreement, brought to his lips statements that were more categorical than I could have hoped: "Too soon! It is much too soon to pave the way for a general disarmament," he said quickly, while an amused glint came into his eyes. (Evidently

they have sent me a prize fool, he thought.) As he
was to go to Paris some time later to sign a treaty of
"cordial agreement" (*bonne entente* in French) with
Monsieur Georges Bonnet, the German Minister
had agreed to this interview and he talked abun-
dantly, developing two principal themes: "First," he
said, with the air of self-sufficiency without vulgarity
which is his, "I am thoroughly familiar with the
mentality of your compatriots. I have travelled frequently in France since the war, particularly in the
Champagne district, and I have found myself in contact not only with the bourgeoisie and aristocracy
but also with the peasantry. I have questioned a
number of people here and there and one thing appears to me undeniable: the French peasant has not
the slightest desire to fight against Germany and he
thinks that the difficulties existing between the two
countries and those which will arise once more between them in the future can be solved without having recourse to arms." The Nazi Minister for Foreign Affairs continued for a long time on this
subject, and he stated positively that his opinion
merely confirmed that of the Führer. And while he
spoke, I recognized the refrain, having heard it already from the lips of dozens of German agents. At
the Wilhelmstrasse a state secretary had piped the
same tune for my benefit in the most honeyed key;
after which the chorus was taken up by younger
members of the party, but more brutally. In the
mouths of the latter, "You don't wish to fight," became: "You can't fight, so why continue to threaten
us with doing so? Wouldn't it be better for you to

accept the expansion of Germany without pretend-
ing to protest?" One day in Paris, Friedrich Sieburg
had said to a few friends, with a curious smile:
"Each French department would give up the neighboring department in order to avoid a war."

In short, our love of peace has, little by little,
been interpreted and described by the Nazis as cowardice. Doubtless we were wrong, not in loving peace
—we would be untrue to ourselves if we ceased to
love it—but in expressing our sentiments so frequently and so insistently that the Germans have at
last found in them a sort of invitation to aggression.

By stressing the pacific sentiments of Frenchmen,
Herr von Ribbentrop obviously sought to persuade
his French hearer to repeat to his compatriots that,
indeed, they did not want to fight. "Direct contacts
between France and Germany must be increased,"
added Herr von Ribbentrop. . . . "And be sure to say
that the only loser at Munich is Russia, and that it
was she, and she alone, who wanted war. . . . And say
also that Daladier was found congenial. . . . Ah!
What a pity that France and Germany did not 'talk
together' as early as 1933. . . . However," he concluded, "repeat that I am optimistic: There will be
no war *if* the men of good will remain in office."

He paused, for a secretary brought him an urgent
message; not a secretary in a tailcoat but another
S.S. in uniform who clicked his heels and raised his
arm in martial salute to a chief—and in the highly
unmartial setting of the hotel hall. After this interruption, Herr von Ribbentrop with ease took up his
discourse where he had left off: "Yes," he continued,

"France and Germany will not fight, *but* France should modify her policy regarding Russia. How can a country as civilised as yours preserve such close ties with the U.S.S.R.? If Paris once and for all repudiated all pacts with Moscow, then uneasiness could no longer subsist between France and Germany and all causes for conflict would be definitely removed." The paragraph concerning Russia seemed of special interest to Herr von Ribbentrop and he asked me to give it particular importance in reporting his statements! "Schmidt (this was the *Gruppenführer* secretary) could look the text over with you, regarding this passage," he said. The minister remained in the hall for a very long time after this; he never went to bed before three or four o'clock in the morning and he rose late: his hours were modelled on those of the Führer.

In the train that took me back to Paris I read over my notes and realized that to publish this interview exactly as it had been given amounted purely and simply to committing an act of Nazi propaganda. Of course this was impossible. When in August, 1939 Herr von Ribbentrop flew to Moscow I realized that beneath the Minister's frigid mask lurked a decided tendency to mystification, a tendency which is, however, praiseworthy in a diplomat. He is a hoaxer, but a serious one. And it was precisely Herr von Ribbentrop's soberness that had struck many a Londoner a few years earlier. When Lady Oxford asked him once whether the Führer ever had moments of relaxation, and if he had any idea of fun, the German Ambassador replied imperturbably:

"The Führer has a great sense of humor. . . ."

"Really? Do give us an example."

"Well, when I tell him a funny story he rolls on the floor with laughter. . . ."

"Ah! So that's what you call humor," murmured Lady Oxford. A little later, she hauled her visitor over the coals, declaring that it was really outrageous for a civilized country to burn the books of one of its writers when that writer was called Heinrich Heine.

"You mustn't understand," replied Herr von Ribbentrop, "we consider that Heine's poetry is not sufficiently *constructive.*"

In the train that brought me back to France after my interview with the German Minister of Foreign Affairs, I met a brother journalist who was returning from another part of Germany. He also had the impression that the Nazis were preparing to strike a heavy blow in the very near future. After crossing the frontier, we looked together at the first French villages. Children were singing on the roads and we could see bellicose . . . billiard players gesticulating behind the glass fronts of little cafés. Nowhere a single uniform. No constraint could be read on any face, nothing mechanical or stiff in people's gait, in fact it was a country of independent, happy, pacific men who were completely indifferent to what went on outside their little paradise. Our hearts felt very heavy. For it was true that if anyone had questioned this peasant or that workman (who looked as though they had wandered out of a film by René Clair) they probably would have said that they had not the slightest desire to fight Germany.

And now that these same Frenchmen are mobilized, they declare that "they have no hatred for Germany." This has just been told me by Captain H. who has just returned from Alsace; he is one of those chiefs before whom soldiers speak freely. At first I felt this declaration was extremely noble, and then I wondered whether a certain degree of absurdity did not underlie such generosity of spirit. For, after all, have the French left their wives, their children, their towns, their countrysides or their business to express themselves like adepts of the Oxford Movement? Before the War of 1914, a Catholic author wrote some considerations on the subject which were very often quoted in colleges during hostilities; these considerations were the cause of much controversy. Roughly, Charles Péguy said this: "Everything must be done to prevent a war, but once one has been forced to fight, well, one must fight." Was not Péguy right?

Does not extreme nobility of sentiment on the part of combatants finally react against the security of the country? And perhaps it is because France is too highly civilized that her war morale is so often ill-assured. Love of peace, of culture, etc., has come to blunt the tough side of our character, the very toughness which democracies must possess (as well as others) when they have to fight. No one can fight without anger, and anger is almost unknown to combatants at present.

DECEMBER 2D

Russia has attacked Finland. . . . But at the Chamber of Deputies, to which I escorted two American journalists this morning, quite different matters were discussed. The Government asked the House for full powers for the duration of hostilities and the deputies rather hesitated to give them. In the lobby Léon Blum declared: "The House convenes for the first time since the war and it is asked to . . . abdicate. . . ." It is very significant that every time a difficult period has to be weathered, the Government is obliged to exact full powers from the House. This sort of thing never happened before 1914. Can it be that since the appearance of dictatorships certain authoritarian dishes are inscribed under assumed names on the menu card of democratic regimes? For full powers means dictatorship in very small doses and under camouflage . . . Or else, have certain problems taken a character of absolutely unprecedented intensity, requiring hard and rapid solutions—the financial problem and the foreign problem, for instance?

During the session, Blum made a declaration of his principles to explain why he would refuse full powers to the Government: "France is waging, with courage and constancy, a war which has been forced upon her. Workers are doing their whole duty towards this war. We are convinced, on our part, that by defending the prerogatives of Parliament we are contributing to maintain the power of France." To underline the importance of this declaration he strained his voice, as he often does. However, the house was completely apathetic and one's impression was that each party continued to adopt such and such an attitude in obedience to a very ancient scenario, but that conviction was lacking, to the right as well as to the left of the Assembly. The Socialists refused Daladier the powers, knowing perfectly well that a War Government needs these powers, and the parties of the majority decided to grant Daladier these powers, without manifesting the least enthusiasm for him. The beneficiary of this measure, the prime minister, did not appear over-eager to obtain what he had demanded, and made a rather feeble speech. (One of my American companions asked me if Daladier was what was called a great orator.) "We are at war," said Daladier, "we are face to face with governments who can act rapidly and with secrecy." To make this discovery on the 1st of December, 1939 is not to find out much of a novelty. For the last six years the Third Reich has had the ability of acting "rapidly and with secrecy" and French diplomats and journalists residing in Germany have sent in report after report on this subject. . . . The government obtained full powers by 318 votes against 175.

I overheard the following remark, made by a deputy in the lobbies of the House: "To think that if we lived in *normal times,* the elections would be

taking place six months from now!" This remark
explains the morose temper displayed by the people's
representatives, who find themselves *frustrated* by
the war and have the impression that very little
importance is attached to what they do or say.
I met V., a deputy who has just been mobilized and
who happened to be in uniform. "My colleagues,"
he told me, "have asked me one thing only, since I
arrived from the front to spend twenty-four hours
with them. . . . They don't say: 'How are we going
to win the war?' or: 'Is the soldiers' morale good?'
No, they repeat: 'What effect have the measures of
exclusion that we have taken against Communist
deputies had upon the soldiers?' And in retrospect
they look terrified while they question me on the
subject which they have so much at heart. They evidently fear that certain leftist electors will remember these measures at the next general elections. . . .
For they continue with the same fixed idea as during
peace time: re-election. . . . I answered that at the
front the soldiers don't care a damn for what might
happen right now to certain Communist deputies.
And that," continued V., "is the opinion even of
troopers who are Communists. And I told my colleagues so all the more freely, as I am a Socialist
deputy. . . . And it was one of my greatest surprises
at the front to discover that opinions had lost a great
deal of their importance and that soldiers had become non-political, that what counted for them now
was whether they could find water here or straw
there; and above all, a grand feeling of solidarity
and fraternity prevails over everything else. . . ."

DECEMBER 4TH

"After all, Hitler is not so remarkable. He is simply the last expression of the Prussian spirit of military domination. . . . His aim is the same as Bismarck's and Wilhelm II's: to dominate Europe." Who speaks thus? A French reactionary? No, an English minister. War time affords the only moments for certain eternal traits of German character to appear in full daylight.

The task of a Franco-British liaison committee is to unify French and English propaganda in Germany. Maurois has left this committee, where he rendered great services, and I have been called upon to replace him. The English delegation is headed by Noel Coward. The first thing I ascertained was that no cooperation had been prepared before the war. From lack of any trustworthy doctrine, the tendency and number of tracts and broadcasts in German are settled empirically. We don't seem to be able to come to an agreement on certain fundamental principles, and when we do succeed in making decisions, the military authorities still have their word to say. Should the enemy morale be attacked above all by the radio (following the German example) or more especially through tracts? On the French side, we rather incline to the latter method and we write texts which would have incalculable repercussions if Germany were populated by seventy million jurists. Certainly a demonstration of the fact that the German citizen is deprived of his rights is conclusive, and our specialists can be proud of their work: but it is doubtful that a German soldier will ever throw his rifle away on that score. . . . Likewise, since the text of the papal Encyclical has been published in Germany in mangled form, we have condensed the full letter into a booklet and our planes will shower the Catholic banks of the Rhine with the words of His Holiness Pope Pius XII. . . . Unfortunately, the reading time of this pamphlet is at least twenty-five minutes, and it is doubtful whether many Germans will be able to peruse His Holiness' noble discourse to the end, all the more so as a tract is a dangerous object which must be hidden and which cannot be consulted at leisure, like a bedside book. As a matter of fact, both outer pages of the pamphlet should have two or three short, striking sentences printed across them in very large characters; these phrases would be easily impressed upon the memory and would have the advantage of being seen several yards off. So the passerby who for obvious reasons would not dare stoop to pick up the tract, could in one sidelong glance take in some essential facts. A short, easily retained formula is as necessary in a propaganda tract as in an ordinary advertisement.

But our principal effort should be brought to bear upon the radio. A text to read is good, but a voice to hear is always far better. Unfortunately, while the

British on our committee can avail themselves of the B.B.C., the Commissariat of Information cannot make use of the French State Radio as it should be able to do. Giraudoux has pleaded, beseeched, implored, but in vain. The other evening, when he alluded to the enormous obstacles which are constantly strewn over his path, someone said to him with a smile: "You must no longer be Girau-*doux* (*doux* means soft), but Girau-*dur*" (*dur* means hard).

DECEMBER 6TH

Yesterday went to the Ministry of War to ask Daladier's assent to the plan for a single joint Franco-British propaganda leaflet. A very quick answer is required, but the Prime Minister already seems buried under mountains of papers. He has allowed himself to be submerged by too much work and is unable to cope simultaneously with the mammoth departments which he has undertaken to control (War, Foreign Affairs); he undergoes periods of great discouragement. And there is something very distressing in a man bowed down under the weight of his own legend, when he also has to face probably the most difficult circumstances that France has ever known. . . . He seems very lonely, almost solitary, and it is more and more difficult to make him decide anything promptly. Several times in his career, he has followed excellent impulses as, for instance, when he decided at the end of 1938, after Italian provocation, to visit Corsica and Tunisia in person. But when he gets to thinking over something, there seems to be no end to his cogitations.

DECEMBER 8TH

I find that the French do not often possess what Marshal Lyautey called "team-work loyalty." If one department asks for something, the department next it is bound to oppose the demand, or else military authorities will refuse to grant a civilian request, or again, one ministry is at daggers drawn with another. . . . In our Hotel Continental live two enemy brothers, Information and Censorship: Cain is represented by censorship.

And yet, since the days of the cathedrals we have erected many great things, thanks to team-work loyalty. . . . Unfortunately, it would appear in recent years that the man who commands, no matter who he may be, is instinctively mistrusted; this sentiment has developed to such an extent that it radically hinders the team from being formed. . . . When, some time ago, I heard Marshal Lyautey bitterly exclaim: "Ah! Offices. . . . If I had remained in France, they would have prevented me from doing anything at all. I made Morocco in spite of the offices." I did not understand in full measure the great soldier's words. The general notion of a final result to be obtained is evidently a notion that does not inhabit the brains of certain officials; on the other hand, these men seem dominated by one pre-occupation: to prevent too many events from happening, too numerous decisions from being taken, for they would multiply boomerang comebacks and thus entail too many risks.

I notice the same reactions in several of the retired diplomats working in the Propaganda Department. However, a diplomat is defined as one who must prevent things from happening, and he triumphs when he has blocked the way to an event of real consequence—war. It remained for dictatorships to create the novelty of the dynamic diplomat—and the followers of our diplomatic traditions have not yet recovered from their surprise. An ambassador who knew his "business" thoroughly was a person who was a trifle overconscious of his own importance, perhaps, and under some aspects rather comical; he would express himself in a most particular jargon; but just the same he remained the son of a superior civilization. Thanks to the gentlemen in frock coats and monocles who met from time to time around a table covered with green cloth, the rhythm of catastrophes remained rather slow and the relative happiness of humanity greatly benefited. Whereas, now that the totalitarian ministers of foreign affairs put on top boots and wear daggers in their belts, they have but one thought: to make the world run faster and faster, to course more and more madly

over the highroad of changes. The sensation caused
by sudden action, and action for the sake of action,
interests them far more than success itself. For no
sooner have they won a victory, than, instead of
consolidating it or profiting from it, as Bismarck
would have done, they fling themselves head fore-
most into new adventures which overthrow still
more frontiers and lead still more people in the infernal dance of revolutions and war. . . . So one
cannot help but feel that the imposing conquests
of the Third Reich present something precarious
and artificial: the tree is tall but has no roots. This
has all grown up in a few days and will perhaps
drop to pieces in the same short space of time.

DECEMBER 10TH

Every day the war destroys some old illusion. In
peace time, perhaps, ideas can be adopted without
being thoroughly examined, while under the test of
fire any idea is completely purged of any doubtful
element that it might contain. And many deep-
rooted principles of yesterday are today revealed to
be fiddlesticks.

So it was repeated to us for years that Germany
must be "given an egress" and everything would be
all right. Sententious gentlemen used yet another
figure: a safety-valve must be found for Germany,

they said, if we don't wish to see her explode. . . .

The funny side of the situation was that when the means of preventing the German explosion had to be found, everyone had different opinions. Poland said to herself that as long as Germany coveted Austria or Czecho-Slovakia, she had nothing to fear. In 1935, Baron Aloisi, an Italian diplomat of the old school and an extremely subtle man, whispered in a visitor's ear that Germany should be allowed to expand towards the East. Many keen wits then wrote to Paris, doubtless in good faith but in a tone that admitted of no reply, that Germany sought *expansion* and not war. This indeed was a most subtle distinction. These thinkers would have done far better had they meditated upon an answer made by our ambassador to Berlin, one day before the 1914 War. When he was asked for the thousandth time: "Does Germany want war?" Monsieur Jules Cambon replied: "No, Germany does not want war." He added imperturbably: "She only wants the fruits of victory."

After the signing of the Munich agreement, sophists (or German agents) did not fail to repeat: "Now, you see, it is just as we have always said, the Nazis do not want to plunge Europe into a bath of blood."

Only now is it understood, everywhere in France, that Nazi Germany was inevitably directed towards war, as a river flows towards the sea. Once in 1938 Herr von Ribbentrop observed to a Balkan diplomat: "Do you suppose that we have acquired arms such as ours, at the cost of billions, for the sole purpose of letting them rust?" This remark was full of

common sense and events have proved its accuracy.
For those who indulge in the risky and dangerous
sport of making political predictions, only the most
obvious factors must be taken into consideration.
If too many elements are introduced into the
problem, they cause a confusion of issues and the
"guesser" is invariably wrong.

This being so, it would take a wise man to ven-
ture, even by faithfully following the essential factor
recipe, the smallest prophecy concerning the direction that events are about to take.

DECEMBER 11TH

The censorship would not pass an article by General Walch. The excesses of censorship are manifest:
instead of restricting itself to suppressing whatever
could help the enemy, it transforms itself into a
machine to protect the government or the High
Command. And so it is that the role of the censor is
a terribly thankless one, and even genius could not
solve the difficulties of the profession and please
everyone at the same time. In order to avoid sinning
from lack of severity, the censors sin through excess.
But in exoneration it must be said that as soon as
they begin wielding their dread scissors, they are
told what happened in 1870; a newspaper appearing
in eastern France printed on its back page an innoc-

uous article containing a sentence about troop movements—and this little sentence was caught by the
enemy and made us lose a big battle.

As a rule, it is General Duval (of the *Journal* and
the *Journal des Débats*) who is persecuted the most,
for he does not think very highly of General Gamelin's talents. The article by General Walch which
was in danger of being suppressed was entitled: "Defensive tactics alone cannot obtain a decision." (A
title which, without appearing too much so, was a
lesson.) The indicted text was addressed to neutrals
and made it understood that the Franco-Belgian
military problem which a German invasion might
propound now at any time had been pathetically
solved, or rather, had not been solved at all. King
Leopold, from highly elevated reasons, perhaps, but
absurd ones none-the-less, abides by an absolutely
neutral policy which may end in consequences as
disastrous for him as for us; and France bows to his
decision. Here are the passages from General Walch's
demonstration, destined for reading beyond our
frontiers and having what Headquarters saw as
thinly veiled reproaches: "From the terrain circumscribed by the network of fortifications and the disposal of blanket troops, the resolution to be guarded
should everywhere be manifested and everywhere
with the same vigilance, as much against the most
loyal neighbor as against the neighbor who only
awaits the opportunity to commit an act of aggression. The result is a linear disposal, all along the
frontier, of forces very unlikely to be capable of
efficient defence. Besides, as regards the shape of

frontiers, it frequently happens that the neutral country is the enveloped and its powerful neighbor the enveloper. If the latter has a heavy appetite and few scruples, he finds in this possibility of encirclement an added facility, and he is tempted to settle the unfortunate neutral's account in the shortest time possible through rapid and powerful mechanical means.

"Thus the isolation to which the neutrals condemn themselves, far from being a protective measure, exposes them, one after the other, to certain destruction. Their best interest should incline them to form an association among themselves and with others."

"It is true that the defensive alone cannot obtain a decision, and we are too Maginot-minded to take the offensive," screams Captain Berthier after reading General Walch's article. And a few hours later, quite by chance, a friend showed me this remark of Voltaire's: "The spirit of peace alone conceived the Great Wall. It is certain that China, governed by laws, merely wished to stop the Tartars who knew nothing but brigandage." China was Maginot-minded, too.

DECEMBER 12TH

Another meeting of our Franco-British Committee. It was asked whether Monsieur Daladier had

given his assent to the plan which had been suggested for a common propaganda leaflet; I am
obliged to say that no decision has yet been taken.
What I don't say is that this answer will be awaited
indefinitely, like everything else. The Prime Minister has announced, for instance, that he was going
to transform our Commissariat of Information into
a ministry, but the days go by and nothing of the
sort happens. Giraudoux, who sees his authority
diminished by this news, waits with his collaborators
for something that never happens.

Had a long discussion with the English on the
following point: should we, in leaflets and over the
air, frankly make an appeal for revolution in Germany? Or else, on the other hand, use threats indif-
ferently towards all Germans, as though they were
all Nazis? The latter proposal finds a good many
adherents—among the same men, however, who
favored publishing articles in the French press on
the necessary dismemberment of Germany after
victory. But we know that these articles were immediately quoted by Dr. Goebbels to prove to the
German people that if their country were defeated it
would lose its unity; according to neutrals recently
returned from Germany, these quotations have rallied to the Nazi regime and its war (in spite of
themselves) many Germans who are indifferent or
hostile to Hitler.

Why count our chickens before they are hatched?
Why talk about what Germany will be after victory,
as though the problem to be solved were the same as
in the eighteenth century? The question will not

even be posed under the same conditions as in 1918, and it is absolutely useless to point out at this time that we will do this or that. It would be far better to insist upon the means in our possession which will allow us to obtain a decision; and upon the possibility, thanks to airplane bombardments, to acquaint the Germans with something they have not known for over a century: war in their own country.

A curious detail: Several of the leaflets thrown by our planes over the large Rhineland cities were, by order, picked up by very young boys belonging to the *Hitlerjugend,* so that the population should not see the said leaflets. But afterwards some of these crafty scamps sold the pamphlets to people as curiosities, at 25 pfennigs apiece.

DECEMBER 13TH

Met M. who also works at the Commissariat of Information and who quite perfectly represents the type of young intellectual with anarchist sympathies who flourished around 1930. He used to show the most profound contempt for public affairs, saying: "Our regime? Doubtless pretty rotten, like all political regimes, but may it last as long as possible and leave me in peace to attend to other matters. But if one of these days we are forced into another little "war for right and liberty," well, I'll say to the gendarmes who bring me my mobilization orders: 'Thank you, gentlemen, but I'm not your man, I'm not interested in this business,' etc. . . ."

However, a few years later M. ceased perusing the *Nouvelle Revue Française,* the advanced periodical which had been his only contact with present-day events, and casually opened a newspaper. What he read had such a powerful effect on him that he threw himself into politics. And a few months ago, when his mobilization order reached him, he set out very readily, like everyone else.

M. reminded me of something I had forgotten: In 1932, or thereabouts, we had spent an evening with Marshal Lyautey and had figured as unbearably sophisticated greenhorns. The Marshal had been retired and was champing at the bit. He, "the royalist who had given an empire to the republic," had been recalled from Morocco in the most humiliating manner by the ungrateful Republic; and in the absence of French warships, it was a British squadron that fired the customary salutes when he left Africa, leaving behind him a disconsolate population and the most extraordinary colonial success in contemporary history. . . . But he had not returned to lead a life of leisure. As some slight consolation, he had been appointed High Commissioner of the 1931 Colonial Exposition and this exposition was a triumph. "I have been appointed . . . custodian of a public square," he used to say. "Now I must amuse myself with sandheaps and make little patties and build pavilions for the exposition, I who have built real cities. . . ." And he often repeated: "My life has been a failure," a most surprising statement, it must be admitted, on the part of a soldier who wore seven stars on the sleeve of his horizon blue tunic.

On the evening that M. recalled to my recollection, the Marshal had spoken about Germany: "A fresh war between France and Germany," he had said, "would be a frightful civil war and our entire European civilisation would perhaps perish in the affray." Next, he discussed the policy which alone, to his mind, could prevent all future conflict: a policy of prestige on France's part: "The stronger we are, the more the Germans will like to work with us and even follow our suggestions. It was not understood at Versailles that we should not have confined ourselves to attempting to prevent Germany from doing damage, we should have associated her in our destiny. . . . We do not realize that Germany, composed, individually, of very virile men, possesses collectively a passive soul. Yes," he repeated, "the Reich would have followed us if we had shown her the way. But instead of finding before her a resolute France, the 'great nation' which she had known, Germany found herself in the presence of . . . a surly usher who never stopped recalling her omissions and failures, who constantly served legal writs on her, and pettifogged and then, giving way to her, squabbled and cavilled in the most niggardly fashion. . . ."

I have thought a great deal about this conversation and also, since the war, have reflected much over the late Marshal, the only great man endowed with a capacity for action that our generation has known. My reason for dwelling on Lyautey is this, that every time French red tape is caught in some particularly flagrant act of non-efficiency, one looks back, by way of consolation, to the example of this Frenchman, who had a real genius for organization. And again, if he possessed as clear a brain as can be found in Descartes' country, Marshal Lyautey also had a dionysiac quality of mind: a very rare blend. He had great precision of conception but he also had an imaginative faculty that allowed him to do things which at the moment seemed mad but were merely on the ladder to the future. When engineers showed him plans for the construction of a port in Morocco, he *saw* what the port would be, and the country, and the wealth of the country ten years later and the proportions which this port should have, and he decided to build a port ten times larger than the one originally conceived. . . . This visualizing faculty he applied equally to big things and small: having founded innumerable cities, he returned to his home in Lorraine and turned Thorey, which did not number five hundred inhabitants, into a sort of model village. "An exemplary cell of France's body," he declared.

Better still: he could spend an entire day making a rough draft of state reforms and then spend as many hours the next day putting the attic of his house in order. However, these tasks in both cases only served to divert him from the great idea of his life—governing France. Lyautey was an example of a very rare vocation: he was born with the convic-

tion that he would one day be at the head of his
country. But although destiny did give him an eminent position, it did not present him with the leading office and nothing could console him for being
second in command; that is why he repeatedly said
that his life was a failure. . . . However, he wished
for power only that he might return France to the
monarchical regime, the only one, he said, which
has given the country an era of grandeur. And this
is where M. and I disagreed with him and found
him retrograde. "The question of a monarchical
restoration is no longer possible in our times, nor
will it ever be," we said categorically. And he
answered: "Wait a little and you will see! This
country has lost its sense of grandeur, and a country
which no longer possesses this sense cannot preserve
its rank for very long. . . . For instance," he added
with brutal frankness, "what strikes me most since I
have returned to Paris is that nobody ever recog-
nizes me in the street." . . . True, Lyautey was one
of the pall-bearers at Marshal Foch's funeral and,
as the procession went by, a spectator in front of
me asked, pointing to Lyautey, "But who is that
gentleman?"

"How many Frenchmen," Lyautey asked, "think
of the French Empire?" He walked up and down in
his office on the Rue Bonaparte, where flags and
pennants from Indo-China, Madagascar and Morocco recalled the stages of his passage across the
continents: "Where are we tending? What is youth
doing?" he enquired. "And first of all, where is this
youth? It looks as though it never let an occasion

go by *not* to show itself. . . . Above all, what is France dreaming about?" M. had answered: "But, Monsieur le Maréchal, France is radical-socialist. . . . And she might die of it! Everyone seeks only to go about his private business in peace."

At these words the Marshal had jumped (the later it grew the more eloquent he became): "I'm not interested in labels or in pigeon-holing political opinions," he replied, "but what is serious is the extraordinary importance given, especially in official speeches, to the adjective *little*. If we believe the political orators, this country is populated by forty-two million average Frenchmen who go to a *little* café for a *little* game of cards before returning to their *little* houses to join their *little* families and read *Le Petit Parisien.*" [1] The idea of grandeur transposed into politics was repugnant to M. and myself. We thought that a government which begins by founding its power on prestige ends by being forced to insure its power by military expeditions and san-

[1] The Marshal hated the state of mind reflected by the *Postman's Almanach.*

> Ma femme tricote
> Sous le lustre près du feu
> Moi je lis un peu
> Et ma fille pianote. . . .
> Gardez nous ainsi, mon Dieu!

Translation:

> My wife knits
> Under the chandelier, near the fire
> I read a little
> And my daughter strums on the piano. . . .
> Keep us thus, oh Lord!

He kept saying: "We did not build an empire by staying by the fireside, with our feet in our slippers!"

guinary victories. We said to the Marshal: "The ideal of grandeur leads sooner or later to war." But he replied: "Not in France, for France has all she needs and in consequence does not have to be imperialistic. But the Republic, in refusing to see things on a grand scale will find out how much this will cost her. . . ." On leaving Rue Bonaparte, M. and I decided, with the assurance of youth, that the Marshal was an amazing man, but that his ideas were decidedly survivals from another age. . . . And yesterday, M. said to me: "After all, contrary to what we thought, the 'Old Man' was a better prophet than we. Indeed, I understood what the absence of grandeur was, the day I saw Daladier, in the motion pictures, arriving at the Munich Conference. . . ." This observation is all the more curious coming from M., who has held what are called advanced ideas.

DECEMBER 15TH

Great agitation at the Ministry of Finance before Reynaud's last speech. Several of the minister's collaborators asked him to soften some of the statements which he wished to make, because they were like whip-lashes in the average Frenchman's face. The "Boss," however stood firm on almost all points, repeating: "Yes, you're afraid that I won't be re-elected in my constituency. However, you must believe me: Facility equals Popularity, but Courage equals Success." After which he stated, a trifle bitterly, that he was unpopular for the time being, but that he would not cease doing what he considered essential; that Daladier had perhaps given him the Ministry of Finances to "sink" him in public opinion, but that he had known the risk of accepting this post and, finally, that he was also quite aware that the taxpayer is like the elephant and never forgets taxes levied. . . . "Too bad, but I can't help it," he concluded.

Reynaud is evidently in an ever-increasing state of exasperation from being right and from a growing desire to show this in punishing the incredulous. And at the same time he holds to the deep-seated conviction that the tide will at last turn in his favor, and that one day the mass of people will recognize his courage and will like him.

Here are the interesting passages in this much discussed speech, which, however, did not produce all the effect on public opinion expected: "Chancellor Hitler puts his stakes on the weakness of democracies and, so far, he has always won. Today his stakes still are on this weakness. . . . The French, he thinks, will spend their time quarreling over the inequality of sacrifices. . . .

"We have adopted the policy of sacrifices not from a taste for unpopularity, but because it is written down in facts. The morale of the country will be preserved if everyone knows that it is along the path of sacrifices that one goes to victory, while one treads the way of defeat on the highroad of facility. . . .

"The democracies will win but at the price of sacrifices of which they perhaps have no conception yet. If we do not enter the fight prepared for everything, it is easy, it is very easy to lose the war. Then, one may ask, are we going to borrow from Germany a regime that is profoundly repugnant to us? What difference will there be between us?

"I answer that the difference will not be in the intensity of effort or in the immensity of renunciation. The difference will lie in one fact, the fact that a free parliament, deciding in the name of a free people, will accept the necessary policy.

"It is possible that this war, which begins in a sort of apathy, will end in a general conflagration; perhaps our ideal of liberty will then exist only at the bottom of our hearts, but it will live, ready to expand after victory.

"We will win, but to vanquish the enemy we must first vanquish ourselves."

The sentence concerning *apathy* was the one which Reynaud's advisers had hoped to suppress, but it was finally left in the speech. Alas, it was received with . . . apathy.

DECEMBER 19TH

Since the British forced the crew of the *Graf Spee* into scuttling their ship, the anti-English propaganda conducted by the Germans, which has proved so devastating, now enjoys little success. The same people who repeated indignantly, "The English occupy the best hotels at La Baule and get one hundred francs pay a day," or again, "And then, they take tea at five!" (The scandal caused by the British army's *five o'clock tea,* by the way, dates from the last war.) today greet one with the words "Have you read the news? They certainly have command of the seas after all. . . ." Nothing succeeds like success—and those who yesterday admired the Germans for the points they have scored in the last few years have had a change of feeling, now that the German Navy has suffered a reverse. And at the same time, the fact that the British take risks, attack and sail dangerously near enemy broadsides gives the lie to the German fable that the English hate to fight and are using the French as mercenary troops.

At the Commissariat of Information, someone remarked that it would be a good idea to show Parisians their allies, to have some sailors march through the streets, for instance, or some of the R.A.F. aces. . . . For up to the present, Parisians have seen scarcely any English, as privates are not allowed to come to the capital on leave. . . . But this suggestion was spurned as too "theatrical."

And yet, General Gamelin said the other day, very justly: "As long as the war has not entered an active phase, Giraudoux's task is more important than mine. . . ." But no one, or scarcely anyone thinks thus and sees the importance of propaganda.

And the importance of the radio is underestimated

in France by officials and politicians; however, they
do admit that Hitler has conquered Germany with
a single weapon: the microphone.

The same state of mind, the same complete ignorance of the advertising methods that can be used
in a modern country, explains the answer recently
made by the Commander in Chief of the air forces.
He was asked for permission to publish the names
of aviators who had brought down several enemy
planes, and this proposal was once more rejected,
with the following explanation: "Pilots must not
be treated as though they were movie stars. This
is not a war of matinée idols."

In short, decisions such as these—and many others
—contribute towards making this war a completely
abstract war, and the French are deprived both of
news and of emotions. This is probably one of the
reasons for the "apathy" mentioned in Reynaud's
speech. . . . As concerns foreign countries, this en-
tails very unpleasant consequences, too. Raoul de
Roussy de Sales, the Frenchman who understands
the United States with his heart as well as with his
mind, writes me from New York that the number
of newspaper lines devoted to our country grow
fewer every day, and that if this goes on much longer
we will be submerged, sunk in oblivion or indifference, we will become a sort of Atlantis. . . .

Turned over a few pages of this journal and
discovered that the war has a predominant place
in it. On the other hand, if I go back ten years I
find scarcely one allusion to public events in what I
jotted down. . . . And then, little by little, the coun-

try's share of important events (that is, the events that are driving it closer to peril every day) has increased—and now a Frenchman's diary is, perforce, the *Diary of France.*

DECEMBER 23D

A rather embarrassed speech in which Daladier declared that in the past it had been impossible to devote considerable sums both to war materiel and to fortifications. That means that the State has been obliged to give priority to one of the two tasks and that the work of fortifications was at first undertaken with more activity. The result of this is that serious gaps have occurred in the production of war materiel, and it has not been possible, it seems, to finish certain orders in 1939 which according to pre-established plan should have been ready by 1940. So, the miracle of gaining a year cannot be performed? How wonderful it would be if, for once, our democracy could be ahead of schedule (as dictatorships unfortunately seem to be, most of the time) and never late. . . . The only assurance given by the Prime Minister is that the fortifications have been built and that some new ones have even been erected since the beginning of the war. For the entire French Army, he declared, is at work, preparing concrete, creating second and third positions. The High Command had told us some time ago that the thing was finished, and the Minister of War says merely that it is being done. . . . We will not dwell on the matter.

The increase in war materiel which is needed will doubtless take a great deal of time. Yet there are only nine hundred and fifty thousand men working in armament factories, whereas in 1918 there were a million and a half.

DECEMBER 24TH

A great many soldiers have been given leave for Christmas and many tables reserved in the restaurants. . . . Statistics have been published at just the right moment so that those who wish to do so may enjoy themselves without suffering too much remorse. It seems that our losses at the end of November were fewer than two thousand men killed and were lower than British casualties at sea. The victims of the war can be set down as follows:

Army	1136	dead
Aviation	42	"
Navy	256	"
Total	1434	"

DECEMBER 25TH

Daladier's eloquence is evidently accessible to all, and his Christmas-Day speech represents the kind of address which appeals most to the soul of the average Frenchman. In contrast with Giraudoux' eloquence, it is what might be described as "omnibus" eloquence. In Daladier's harangues we have a combination of simplicity, banality, softened pride, emotion, southern gravity and good-fellowship which obtain an unfailing success. At the moment when peasant women in their cottages and the defenders of the Maginot Line listen favorably to the Prime Minister, he sees his prestige decrease in an alarming manner at the Chamber and in certain well-informed Parisian circles. The war in Finland is the cause of his waning credit. The controversies provoked by the Russian aggression grow more venomous every day and the censorship is obliged to allow some of the more violent articles to appear.

It has always been so during recent years: one allows oneself to drift towards such or such a line of conduct regarding foreign policy, solely through party spirit. Out of hatred for Bolshevism, for instance, the immediate despatch of an expeditionary corps is demanded. But the Scandinavian countries won't allow it to pass through their territory. Very well, our troops must disembark at Narvik, the amateur strategists decide, as if this were the simplest thing in the world, a little excursion. At the same time, it does not seem to occur to them that the war against Germany continues and that the Nazis remain our principal enemies.

DECEMBER 28TH

"Once more I ask whether it is possible for France, in the Europe of today, to maintain her standard of living, to arm herself for defense and to rest two days a week?" This is part of a speech made by Reynaud twelve months ago—and remains true.

JANUARY 11, 1940

Racine, Marivaux, are played at the Comédie-Française; as in other years, the Goncourt Prize has been awarded; candidates for the Académie Française come forward. . . . In the midst of war, literature continues to play a part in the private life as well as the public life of the French—to the surprise of foreign observers. The other day, a minister made a speech about rationing: the harangue contained a quotation from Victor Hugo and one from Renan. One of the things that most surprised German journalists who attended parliamentary sessions before the war was to hear, for instance, Monsieur Caillaux quote a stanza by Verlaine in the course of a discussion on the budget; or the President of the Army Commission refer to Anatole France. The Socialists were not annoyed that Monsieur Blum knew Stendhal by heart, nor the Communists that Aragon had been a surrealist; very much the contrary. In his book *Towards a Professional Army,* General de Gaulle brings Paul Valéry into his argument, and Reynaud, speaking of municipal reforms to be carried out in Marseilles, calls Chateaubriand to the bar. . . . Even at electoral meetings, literature is called upon for a generous contribution, just as in the Montmartre cabarets or in the *Canard enchaîné.* . . .

When George Moore returned to Paris a few years ago, he was asked: "What surprises you most?"

He answered: "That nothing has changed. Thirty years ago, when I reproached the coachman of a *fiacre* for his horse's slowness, he replied:

Qui veut voyager loin ménage sa monture [1]

And yesterday, when I tried to run after a bus and missed it, the conductor stopped the car for me and, like the coachman, borrowing La Fontaine's voice, said:

Rien ne sert de courir, il faut partir à point [2]

[1] La Fontaine. ("He who wishes to travel far spares his nag.")
[2] La Fontaine. ("It serves little to run, a timely start is best.")

However, if our authors continue to assert themselves at all, they reflect the war, for the most part,
in their writings. They do this spontaneously; they
have enlisted in this work; it has not been necessary
to mobilize them. The events of the day inevitably
cast their shadows over everything, even over poetry,
and this changes many things. The other day at the
Comédie-Française, when the bard Racine had sung
his verse, the *Marseillaise* was played, as it is played
at the end of every performance now. . . . Rouget
de l'Isle's rugged voice following Racine's musical
accents—what a lesson! Whether we wish it or not,
the peril of our fatherland shows its presence everywhere. . . . One of the results of the Hitlerian ascent
in Europe will be to threaten considerably the de-
velopment of literature for literature's sake. The
growing concern over the country's defence greatly
reduces the chances of cultivating the ego.

As a result, the "vanguard writers," as the public
calls them, raise very few new recruits, while the
most seasoned of these authors no longer know which
saint (or which demon) to call to their assistance.

An example of this is Cocteau, who during the
war wanted to write a play in which the war was not
mentioned, and he has not been able to produce the
play which he would have written in normal times;
and his *Monstres Sacrés* which is being shown now,
is a miscarriage. . . . Politics determine the nature of
the mind's creations and it is not, as we used to say
in our youth, the intellectuals who influence the
course of politics. Or if they do have an influence
over politics, it is far weaker than they believe. . . .

Hitler's accession to power in 1933 coincides more or less exactly with the close of the extremely brilliant literary epoch in France which began in 1919. Indeed it has been remarked that the post-war period ended in 1933. The present war will mark the break even more sharply, and a new expression of French thought will be revealed; but up to now we cannot have the least idea of what it is to be. The well-known authors of 1938 will then suddenly acquire a historical value and will have great difficulty in keeping an audience among the youth. But there will always be authors in France, just as there will always be vineyards on the slopes of Burgundy and the Bordelais country.

JANUARY 12TH

The difficulty in finding any coffee is once more the subject of conversation, probably because there are no other events of greater interest. . . . In fact, there is nothing of importance to mention on our front, and the mass of the public are now so accustomed to a war masquerading as peace that they are beginning to kick, just as they would in peace time. . . . In September people expected an apocalyptical war, and nerved themselves to bear it bravely. And now, since nothing has happened, much grumbling is heard because there is not enough coffee. The roaring of cannons has not been heard, the dreaded destruction has not come to pass—so the public has returned to its habitual thoughts and recriminations —currents of a past epoch, the age of butter which was believed to be dead and gone and which yet survives itself. . . . So much so that the Government has been obliged to publish a communiqué asking people to stop hoarding coffee, and has announced that in another fortnight the stocks will be increased to normal.

In the press, at least as far as the popular newspapers are concerned, the usual news items—daring burglaries, horrible murders, etc.—are on the point of leaping to front page popularity and big headlines. The editor of *Paris-Soir* which had a wide circulation, is sending one of his reporters to America in search of articles which, he says, "will give us a little change from war." The editor in chief of *Le Figaro* received one evening a communiqué which read simply: "A few local engagements of small importance. Foggy, rainy weather over the whole front"; he remarked with a sigh: "How can our readers be interested in war communiqués which sound like weather reports? If this goes on, the war will end on the back pages of newspapers. . . ."

To cheer a population which is still expecting something which never happens, we have been informed that . . . the race tracks will be opened again on February 18th. And the High Command, not being able to publish anything seriously interesting, has asked us to give the papers details of the soldiers' basic rations. Here they are. They are, of course, daily rations:[1]

At the rear			At the front		
Bread	600	grammes	Bread	600	grammes
Vegetables ..	60	"	Vegetables ..	160	"
Sugar	32	"	Sugar	48	"
Salt	20	"	Salt	20	"
Coffee	24	"	Coffee	36	"
Bacon	30	"	Bacon	30	"
Meat	350	"	Meat	400	"
Wine	one pint		Wine.....	a pint and a half	

This does not include soap, tobacco, etc. . . .

In short, everything is being done to persuade soldiers as well as civilians that "the good old times," or what is left of them, have not quite disappeared.

However, rumors of all sorts are in circulation; every one thinks he knows precisely what unforeseen shape Hitler's grand plan will take, or what should be done at once to save the Finns. . . . Sometimes the highly fanciful fables which pass from lip to lip contain some correct detail; or else people allege things which they know to be false in order to get at the truth. . . . For instance, a visitor with an extremely worried face entered my office the other morning and said: "Well, you know what's being said?"

"No," I replied, "what is being said?"

"Why, I don't know, I'm asking you!"

[1] The English pound corresponds to about 450 grammes.

JANUARY 15TH

"It is not necessary to read the whole of *Mein Kampf*," declares a specialist on German questions at the Commissariat of Information, "for this thick, indigestible volume which everyone quotes and which no one has been able to finish, has been summed up for us beforehand in a single line by Victor Hugo:

Europe, dit Berlin, ris! La France n'est plus. . . .
(Laugh, Europe! says Berlin. France is no more)

JANUARY 21ST

New alarm: Belgium and Holland were about to be invaded, but we were quickly informed and considerable troop movements at once took place all along our northern frontier. The Germans did not expect such lightning disposition of troops and, perhaps for this reason, at the last moment cancelled the order of invasion. Some say that this is a "new move in the war of nerves." But this is not probable, considering the importance of the massed German effectives and materiel.

The Commander in Chief's plan is to enter Belgium as soon as Germany invades our neighbors. So there is no doubt but that we will not remain in our fortified positions, as was thought at first; to remain so would have been more in keeping with General Gamelin's idea, which is to keep to a war of position for the time. (And that is why the High Command turned a deaf ear when it was considered attacking the Siegfried Line to help Poland; and when the drawing of a firm and military chalkline against Italy was suggested; and when preparations for important operations in the Near East were advised by General Weygand, etc., etc. . . .)

These many days now, we have been ready to believe that our army would enter Belgium, and some of us could already see our men taking the offensive and debouching in Germany by turning the extremity of the Siegfried Line. . . . The Prime Minister would have been vastly relieved if the Command were to place before him a successful *fait accompli* and was very much disappointed to see that nothing happened. . . . At all events, if the French abandon a "sit down" war for a war of movement when the Germans violate the Low Countries' neutrality, the Command will have made a decision most pleasing to the Army, which is champing at the bit.

JANUARY 23D

The Belgians have again refused the request made
of them during the last state of alarm, that they
come to an understanding with our General Staff on
the measures eventually to be taken for our common
safeguard. And so, a series of articles, purposely
spared by the censorship, concerning the "council"
of high military authorities is now appearing. It is
hinted in these articles that the Albert Canal constitutes a position of some value but one which could
not resist very long; that this artificially fortified line
was made only after refusal on the part of Holland to consider any common military plan of defence for herself and Belgium. For, as a matter of
fact, the Belgians asked the Dutch for the same cooperation as we requested of the Belgians and received the same kind of refusal. . . . "Each man for
himself" such is the great principle, diplomatic as
well as military, which governs Germany's neighbors, that is, her eventual victims. These past few
years, every time a country has been attacked by
Germany, the victim's neighbors have closed their
eyes, stopped up their ears and declared: "This is
not my business." Such an attitude, we were told,
was the realist's attitude, and was alone able to prevent those countries which so courageously closed

their eyes and stopped up their ears, from being dragged into the war.

Now it happens that History has punished terribly those who have put these principles into practice. When Austria was invaded, no one around her moved so much as a finger, and six months later came Czecho-Slovakia's turn: she had previously declared: "Better the *Anschluss* than the Habsburgs." When Czecho-Slovakia was carved up, Poland served as an accomplice in the operation, and one year later *her* turn came. France who, as early as 1936, at the time of the reoccupation of the Rhineland, had refrained from action in order not to create a *casus belli,* was finally compelled to make war when several of her allies had been either strangled or terrorized by Germany, like Belgium, and other neutrals in the Balkans. England, who believed for a long time that peace-time conscription, alliances on the continent, and war, were not for her, finally got one after the other: peace-time conscription, a treaty with Poland, and war. Lastly, all who had been slow in rearming through lack of foresight or lack of courage, or because they wished to economize, or because they thought it better to spend millions on schools and hospitals than on guns, were compelled to spend a sum ten or a hundred times greater than the sum which would have ensured their safety in the beginning.

This "each man for himself" principle is in itself so narrow that it could not be followed for its own sake, no matter how great the propensity among peoples and governments for adopting the stupidest course; but there was another motive, less easy to acknowledge: each neighbor, or possible victim, is secretly terrified. The prevailing conception of strict neutrality actually derives from nothing in the world but fright; since Germany has rearmed, her small neighbors are scared out of their wits. In fact it is as though the neutrals said to France and England: *"Messieurs les gendarmes,* our sympathies are with you, but the highwayman has become, we fear, stronger, better armed and more resolute than you. So please excuse us if we do what he asks, and if we refuse to form a group of neutrals and then join in with you." Blackmail and terror have become the great realities of international policy. For the last four years, these realities have been the key to almost all the events that have taken place in Europe since 1933. . . .

This is nothing new. But since 1919 we had been led to believe that certain practises were no longer allowed in international politics. In our relations with our fellow men, for instance, we may institute a lawsuit, but an armed highway robbery is not admitted as a means of arranging a difficulty. And so we had all concluded that man was progressing and that this progress had been accepted once and for all.

However, if order exists among individuals in society, it exists because of a certain institution called the police. And if we can imagine a society without policemen, order, an artificial state, would at once disappear and the natural state, which is disorder, would return at full gallop. I do not remember who said that decency and security reigned in large cities because certain of the inhabitants were called policemen and put into blue uniforms, but one has only to see the expression of baffled rage on many a face to realize how many things are repressed by order. "And if looks could give life or death, the streets would be full of murdered men and pregnant women." . . .

In relations between nations there has never been an international police to maintain peace. So peace is merely the result of forces which balance one another; as forces vary every day, constantly, the question of equilibrium has to be readjusted. . . . Individuals no longer live dangerously, or as dangerously as they lived in the Middle Ages, for instance—but peoples have always lived and will continue to live dangerously. And the worst thing that can happen to them, to a certain degree, is to be happy, for in their happiness they forget the sword of Damocles which hangs—more or less high, but permanently—over the heads of all nations, great or small. Democracy, in multiplying the chances of individual happiness, is the regime which exposes a people most seriously to forgetfulness or to under-estimation of danger. Democracy does not keep her citizens in a state of tension or constant alarm (this would be contrary to her ideals), but she makes them live in a psychologically mild climate. As man rises in the scale of civilization he is like an animal that loses certain of its natural means of defence, and these fighting weapons, which were indispensable at an earlier stage of the race, are no longer useful: he abandons, one after another, his claws, his fangs, etc. . . .

When one sees our French ministers, badly dressed, smiling, witty (putting things at their best) quite capable of underhand money dealings (this has happened . . .) but fortunately incapable of organizing butchery on a grand scale in the style of the June, 1934 German "purge" or the Russian "super purge" of 1937, one has a distinct feeling of beholding the end of a long historical evolution. . . .

JANUARY 30TH

About two weeks ago, Monsieur Daladier fractured his instep on a horseback ride near Rambouillet. The accident was announced in the newspapers without the fact being mentioned that a horseback ride had caused the mishap, for riding is not one of the things allowed to a French Prime Minister. (Horses have been dishonored in our Republic since one of them all but carried a certain rider, General Boulanger, to a dictatorship.) Since his accident, the Prime Minister's temper has been even more morose than it was before, and he allows urgent decisions to remain in suspense for an even longer time. After the end of November, for instance, the Commissariat of Information was to be transformed into a ministry, and yet this has not come about. M., who is as superstitious as only a Frenchman can be when he once believes in such things, told me that this acci-

dent was an unlucky sign. But he added jestingly:
"The historians of the future will write that Monsieur Daladier's rule was divided into two parts: 'Before the fracture' and 'After the fracture,' just as the history of Louis XIV's life was cut into two, after a famous operation: 'Before the ablation of the fistula' and 'After' "!

The Prime Minister was, however, able to make a speech where he used certain information which we sent him about the forms taken by German propaganda. He summed things up in a very simple manner: this simplicity is one of the qualities which André Chamson used to inspire, when he "prepared" Monsieur Daladier's speeches, and it still subsists in the Prime Minister's speeches although André Chamson is no longer by the side of his "boss." "German propaganda," declared Monsieur Daladier, "says to the rich: 'You are going to lose your money.' It says to the workman: 'This war is a war of rich men.' It says to the artist, to the intellectual: 'All that you love is threatened with destruction.' It says to those who love the good things of this world: 'A few months more and you will have to accept the hardest of restrictions.' It says to the man who has religious beliefs: 'Can your faith accept these massacres?' Finally, it says to the adventurer: 'A man like yourself can carve himself a place in the misfortunes of his country.' "

Yes, this propaganda puts money on every horse; this is its whole policy and one of the reasons, I think, for its success.

Up to the present, foreign propaganda had a

limited scope. The U.S.S.R., for instance, is there to "stir up" the working man, above all, the peasants a little and certain intellectual circles, a very little. It may be said that its clientèle remains specialised. In the same manner Germany used formerly to reach certain very clearly circumscribed zones of opinion only: before 1914 and from 1918 to 1933 we knew that such and such sectors would be attacked by German agents while others would never be. But the Nazi propaganda is Protean, it takes all aspects imaginable and its motto is: "I am everywhere."

That is totalitarianism applied to propaganda.

This propaganda would have had little effect on "the rich" if they had understood what was taking place in the Third Reich and had realized that the State was capable, there, of being far more of an "inconvenience" to them in certain ways, than in our democracy. But in denouncing Bolshevism for years, the Führer had acquired great sympathy among conservatives who would never in the world have "gone in" for Wilhelm II. Propaganda has succeeded in convincing certain French workmen, ill-informed of what was going on in Germany, that the imaginary "paradise," previously situated in Moscow, was now installed across the Rhine. Artists and the adepts of butter, whom she openly insults in public speeches, Nazi Germany does not bother to seduce with fascinating talk, but she repeats to them the most demoralising arguments. She has persuaded a great number of them that they are anachronisms, the ashes of a dead world, etc. . . .

Finally, leaving no stone unturned and shirking

no difficult tasks, the Third Reich has made appeal after appeal to those Christians who are penetrated with evangelical pacifism—and this long before the war—to make them take a stand against the idea of war *in their country;* yet these Christians are looked upon by Hitlerians as the most despicable individuals, the conscientious objector being considered by the Nazi "hero" the scum of humanity! It is curious, for instance, to see how Nazi Germany has maneuvered the Oxford Movement in England to her own interests.

As far as adventures are concerned, everyone knows how many of the failures among members of the upper classes, among the disappointed flotsam and jetsam, among the corruptible in the political world, are quite ready to play any kind of role under any conditions.

A propos of those in "society," there is one quality which Nazi propaganda has exploited wonderfully: snobbishness. This propaganda has reversed the current of snobbishness.

In past years, snobbishness drifted to the left, indulged all forms of Socialism and Communism. It was then that we saw unforgettable extravaganzas. Lord F. for example, in England, in the castle of his ancestors, used to call for the *Daily Worker* which was brought to him on a silver tray, respectfully tendered to him by a butler. (The same person used to go to Communist meetings in the East End of London, driven in a magnificent almond green Rolls-Royce.) And in Paris there were several princesses who belonged at the same time to the Third International and the Two Hundred Families. There was a time when one "went to Moscow"; it was a smart journey, like a season at Salzburg. And then one day everything changed.

The Nazi "brand," profiting by the interest which is always taken in success, novelty, and powerful technical advertising, stepped in with authority and little by little eclipsed the Soviet "brand." People began going to Berlin, duchesses told how delightful shivers ran down their spines when they heard the Führer roar, etc. . . . After all, the French-Germany Committee received a number of new members, there was much talk of objectivity, sang-froid, open-mindedness, and the rest. Lectures were organised in Paris for Herr Sieburg and Fräulein Leni Riefenstal etc. . . . Quite by chance, or so it seemed, paid journeys for purpose of study were offered, invitations received for the Nuremberg Congress and the Olympic Games in Berlin in 1936. And some non-Aryan ladies (but married to noblemen) went on a pilgrimage to Berchtesgaden, as one goes on a pilgrimage to Bayreuth, while certain Parisian novelists discovered in Germany that they held a considerable place in France and could modify the course of their country's policy.

Why, one might ask, did the Nazis attempt so methodically, after the German fashion, to win over certain men of letters belonging to the left or the right wings of literature and certain smart ladies? Because, contrary to what is commonly thought, the French Revolution was in great part the work of the snobs of the period; and it was seen clearly enough

between 1920 and 1930 how quickly and easily snobbishness formed modish reputations, how, thanks to
snobbishness, artists and movements, from the Russian Ballets to Surrealism, instantly became celebrated.

Here is another side of the question which did not
escape the Germans: a great many women of the
world who are the leaders of Parisian society have
family connections in banking and industry, or else
exert influence over important political men (indeed, the only manner in which our ministers of the
left wing can render homage to the *Vieille France*
is to take, as their Egerias, countesses and mar-
chionesses).

If so many bankers and politicians in France as
well as in England have thought that the policy of
appeasement could calm Hitler, it is because this
idea has often been inspired by ladies spontaneously
transformed into diplomatic advisers. Most of these
women, however, acted for the most part in perfect
good faith, because the ideas which had been wafted
through indirect channels to them from Berlin possessed simultaneously the flavors of subtlety and ir-
resistible profundity, seeming, as they did, to belong
to "higher politics"; and is it not amusing to touch
a little on "higher politics" between a visit to Suzy
and a fashionable charity ball? The typically per-
suasive talk, such as I have heard a hundred times,
runs pretty much as follows: "Of course you understand that *he* is not mad enough to make war. *He*
talks to them the way he does just to keep them in
his power, but *he* wants to obtain great results with-

out bloodshed. If he disappeared, Bolshevism would be established in Germany and immediately afterwards here, in our country. . . . We had far better come to an understanding with *him*, instead of remaining faithful to our alliances with countries in Central Europe whose very names are impossible to remember" (smile), "and which are such an expense to us. . . ." Then as a conclusion, this "wise" sentence: "And then, *he* will not make war, because, first of all, in time of war the German Army would be in command and *he* would find himself playing second fiddle. . . . No, it is not to *his* interest to attack us, etc. . . ."

The Nazi files were well kept: there was not a single socially important household in pre-war Paris upon which siege had not been attempted. And everyone was attacked in a weak spot. Thus Hélène de Portes has been led to believe in the extraordinary importance of her role, since certain messages have been brought to her from Germany by special envoys. In the spring of 1939 she told me that a German woman, who had an introduction from a friend in Berlin, came to tell her—Hélène de Portes —most confidentially that Hitler knew perfectly well how to solve the Franco-German problem: "The Führer is quite aware that there is only one intelligent man with new ideas in the French Parliament: Paul Reynaud. When the day comes that Paul Reynaud is Prime Minister, all questions will be very rapidly solved, for the representatives of France and Germany will be for the first time, and simultaneously, men completely free from prejudices, etc. . . ."

With her astounding assurance, between two shrill laughs, Hélène de Portes repeated: "Five minutes, it will take just five minutes!" I imagine that Reynaud must have smiled a little when this message was given him. That day Hélène de Portes saw the German problem solved in anticipation; then she passed on to something else, without giving the matter another thought. For she jumps continually from one idea to another, without ever fixing her attention on anything for long. And this is what irritates Reynaud's collaborators so much, for they can never foresee in what direction she will influence the minister, when she does influence him. She has no defined policy but merely follows her impulses. And sometimes she favors one thing and sometimes leans towards another, without the least fear of apparent contradiction in her opinions.

At the time of each European crisis, Hitler's conscious or unconscious agents put into circulation a certain number of ready-made opinions. Here are a few examples of what I mean: Before 1938, they repeated incessantly: "The horrors of war are well-known to Hitler, who is a veteran of the last European conflict. He doesn't want another war." After the *Anschluss*, Germany's first aggression, they declared: "Nazi Germany is far too busy *digesting* her success to risk a new adventure." After Munich, they surpassed themselves in craftiness. The refrain which was made up in Berlin to be repeated in Paris and in the provinces was as follows: "Hitler does not want war, otherwise he would have fought instead of signing the Munich Settlement." In 1939, after he entered Prague, they found this, and I quote: "We have invented a new technique in foreign policy, the technique of blackmail, thanks to which we shall obtain everything we want without a war. . . ." Distinguished people fell into this trap. The Rumanian Minister of Foreign Affairs, Mr. Gafencu, who saw Hitler and later came to Paris in the spring of 1939, confidentially told some friends that, in his opinion, the Führer would make use of war threats but not of war. At the same time, German propaganda succeeded in popularizing in France phrases, or words, which disqualified certain Frenchmen, for instance the word: hysterical. Every Frenchman who denounced the German plan was called hysterical. *Sang-froid,* cool-headedness, was the thing most needed, people said.

The common sense of the French was much talked about, so was their confirmed optimism; all this to reassure them, because Nazi Germany wanted to put France and England to sleep *at any price.*

JANUARY 31ST

Letter from Arthur who has been promoted to corporal; he left the depot only two weeks ago and is in Alsace in a quiet sector. However, he writes that from time to time, *il y a bal chez Adolphe* ("Adolf is giving a ball"), which means that the German

lines are being bombarded. His letter swarms with
new expressions, as hundreds of word pictures and
phrases are continually created at the front, highly
picturesque ones for the most part. The Frenchman has a sort of genius for creating unexpected
epithets. For instance, who could have imagined that
the American, Fred Snite, journeying in his "iron
lung" through France, from Paris to Lourdes, should
have struck the popular imagination here so vividly?
Be it as it may, "iron lung" or (*poumon d'acier*) is
the expression used by Arthur and his comrades to
designate their sleeping bags. . . . Arthur says that
he has been given a new uniform which he calls his
"smoking Daladier," and that in his company some
of the boys are *drôlement gonflés*. For *gonflés* and
moustachus are terms used to indicate plucky, brave
soldiers. Those who simply do their work and no
more and keep watch quietly in the rain, covered
with their long caped and hooded coats or *pélerines*
are called *pélerins;* the last word also means pilgrim
and thus provides a pun. It was some time before
I understood one of the passages in Arthur's letter:
"At the canteen," he writes, "there is nothing but
beer, not a single general or the least captain." And
then I remembered that in the curious hierarchy
given to apéritifs in slang, a "captain" is a *mandarin*
and a "general" is a *pernod*. I also recollected with
amusement that at barracks, when Arthur was about
to discuss politics with a comrade, he always began
by saying with supreme elegance, to his opponent:
"Will you allow me, Toto, to unpack my tools?" For
the language of the people, like the more precious

literary styles, has continual recourse to verbal images, and "I unpack my tools" meant "I will expose my arguments."

Arthur is not too homesick for "Paname"[1] but he would have liked to be there on February 15th, when the football season opens, for a big match between the English and the French teams.

FEBRUARY 9TH

During the last secret committee, a deputy, Fernand Robbe, affirmed that we had only eight hundred first line planes. But the Minister of Aviation, Guy La Chambre, declared that we possessed two thousand three hundred machines—this figure strengthened the Assembly's confidence in the Daladier cabinet, but is questioned by many.

FEBRUARY 11TH

The Supreme Council of February 7th, which was the longest of the war, was, it seems, devoted in major part to Finland. Mr. Chamberlain has for a

[1] Paris.

long time, since December in fact, resisted the idea of intervention. Daladier, checked at the same time by the Command and by England, has not been able to act very quickly either, and as a result the opposition found a means of putting him in difficulty before the Chamber. Basically, the deputies are surprised that they gave so much power at the beginning of the war to a man who uses it so timidly, and the uneasiness over Finland only makes the general uneasiness livelier and more precise. I mean the general uneasiness caused by the rapid and continuous decline in the Prime Minister's prestige. (To think that neutral journalists wrote for weeks that French democracy was dead and that Daladier was one more dictator to be added to the list of Führers and Duces!)

When uneasiness reigns in the Chamber during war time, this means that a secret committee meeting is about to be held. And this has just been decided. And as took place during the last war, General Headquarters has persistently asked the Government that a minimum of secrets be divulged to this secret committee. For it is impossible that a secret should be kept by six hundred and eighteen deputies, most of them married, and not to silent women. Reynaud said that a secret cannot be strictly kept even at a council of ministers. And it seems—and this is even more disquieting—that one day Herriot and Campinchi exchanged a few words in a very low voice in the House lobby about a most confidential piece of news, and the next day this news was known in Berlin. . . .

Before the House convened for a secret session—or

so-called secret session—Daladier read a document which showed how much the Germans, in spite of the war, continued to be on the look-out for information concerning French interior politics. On an agent of the Gestapo was found a minutely planned notebook, in which were the following noteworthy questions, in order of priority, to be put to those who would be questioned:

1. How many votes will Daladier obtain?
2. Who are his principal adversaries, acknowledged or secret?
3. Who will be his eventual successor?

It is difficult, however, to give answers to this book of questions, for, long before the war, party labels counted far less than they used to; there remained the party of those who wished to continue the war with energy and the party of . . . the others; the party of the *hard* and the party of the *soft,* both of which are talked about unceasingly.

In the years preceding the war, Nazi propaganda prepared this great simplification: it tore each of our parties in two. For to the right, as well as to the left, there are the *hard* and the *soft.* An American journalist came and asked me this morning for a list of parties, in order to be better informed about them before sending to his paper some considerations on the result of the secret committee. And he was much surprised, on opening a little book, to find that no fewer than nineteen parties in the Chamber were elected in 1936. Split in two by Germany, these nineteen parties have become thirty-eight fractions and even a Frenchman finds this scale a trifle too vast.

According to the almanac which I have by me at present, these nineteen parties are the following:

Conservative Party

Democratic Republican Union Party

Republican Federation Party

Independent Popular Action Party (Alsatians and Lorrainers)

Independent Party of Social Action

Independent Agrarian Party

Popular Democratic Party

Left Wing Republican Party. (Those belonging to the party, it is said, being Republicans but not leftists.)

Democratic Alliance Party

Independent Radical Party

Radical Socialist Party

Socialist Republican Union Party

Independent Leftist Party

Camille Pelletan Party (!)

Frontist Party

Young Republic Party

Proletarian Unity Party

Socialist Party. (Or more exactly, French Section of the Workers' International.)

Communist Party

There is also the fluctuating party of those who belong to no special group or who leave one group for another. . . . This splitting up of groups has increased greatly in recent years.

And groups continue indefinitely to oppose groups, all the more readily as arguments find an easy footing in an assembly where lawyers and intellectuals are generously represented.[1]

And what is more, these groups, in spite of their number, do not even represent fifty percent of the electors; far from it. For first of all, out of the twelve million French voters, about fifteen percent abstain; this means that eighteen hundred thousand voters, through their own fault, might very well not exist. And also, but this time because of a most arbitrary electoral system, the elected represent only five and a half million votes, according to recent calculations; and the votes obtained by defeated candidates, that is, about four million seven hundred thousand votes, count for zero, as in France we do not have *proportionate representation;* so if we add the electors of defeated candidates to the abstentionists we find:

4,700,000
1,800,000

6,500,000, which means that more than 54 percent of the electors = 0.

[1] Professions of deputies:

Lawyers	124
Journalists, men of letters, professors	121
Workmen, employees, artisans	83
Industrialists	49
Merchants	45
Agriculturalists	42
Landed proprietors	42
Doctors	33
Functionaries	30
Divers occupations	48
	617

In other words, when the House sits, only 46 percent of all Frenchmen are represented, according to the present and most imperfect democratic interpretation of the elections. And a government which has a majority of half the Chamber plus one vote, no doubt possesses a parliamentary majority, but in reality it merely groups around itself deputies representing 24 percent of the French.

Attempts have been made to change the system, but on this score—as on others—reforms seem to terrify both right and left of the Assembly. There is a superstitious dread of putting the regime in danger by modifying the electioneering system; and for the same reason women are refused the vote.

FEBRUARY 13TH

General B., who is not very favorably viewed in higher circles because he holds non-conformist opinions on many subjects, is convinced that some blow will be aimed at the front, and a very violent blow. "Then we will see thousands of armored cars hurled against one another and two hours of this war will be worse than two days at Verdun during the last war." He admits that the aggressors' armored cars will find on their road what are called passive obstacles, that they will strike mines, and that the expedition will not constitute a pleasant little stroll. But he adds, "the task of destroying these obstacles will fall to detachments of engineers, using powerful means and handling explosives of considerable potency. However, as soldiers of the engineer corps cannot work under the very eyes of the men who are defending these works, enormous artificial clouds will have to be formed. The battle will evolve thus:

1. The blinding of the occupants of the Maginot works by an artificial fog. Favored by this fog, the destruction by the engineering corps of obstacles hindering the advance of the assailant's tanks.

2. The armored cars, when they have advanced sufficiently, will fire at the casemates.

3. And the corps of engineers, protected by the armored cars which have driven nearer, will continue on and achieve the destruction of the casemates by explosive torpedoes, etc."

Two officers who have just arrived from the front lines declare that the morale is excellent there when the officers have their men well in hand, and that the "human materiel," as the Germans call it, is always capable of great things in our army. These officers are indignant at the "phoney war" idea which prevails at the rear and filters through to foreign countries, for this war is already a very serious thing for hundreds of thousands of men, and the fact that wholesale slaughters have not taken place does not detract from the war's grave character. "Paris (that is, certain people and certain conversations heard only in Paris) once more cloaks not only the army, but France itself," they say. For at the rear, in the country whence the men have gone to the front,

whence the horses have been commandeered, whither
thousands and thousands of refugees have been sent,
the war effort is very great. But instead of under-
scoring the sacrifices already made and asking still
more, instead of stimulating the will to make yet
heavier sacrifices, most of the time one tries ("one"
means political leaders) to reassure public opinion.
A grievous psychological error in the face of the
situation.

The trials of certain families are indeed very great,
and yesterday I was told of the case of Doctor Bidou,
who has eight sons in the army; the last born, a stu-
dent, has just been mobilized; in the Bidou family,
all ranks and all services are represented: a corporal
in the engineer corps, a hospital orderly, an infantry
private, a radio telegraphist in the Maginot Line, a
sergeant in the colonial troops, etc. . . . There is also
a ninth Bidou son, but he has not yet been called
to the colors because a decree allows missionaries
now in Africa to stay where they are.

The two officers also made an interesting observation: they think the announcement of Mr. Sumner
Welles's journey to Europe, with all the comments
it will give birth to and the no less extraordinary
hopes which it must arouse, will probably increase
the uncertainty of most of the population. For even
in war time, shifts of opinion count for a great deal
in democracies such as ours; we remain vulnerable
on this point, whereas the frightful constraint imposed by dictatorships makes autocratic regimes almost completely indifferent to what is said in their
countries. Sir Roderick Jones, of Reuters, told me

once that, receiving Herr von Ribbentrop a few years ago in England and hearing from the latter's lips what the representative of the Third Reich was going to say to the British, he attempted to give the ambassador a little timely advice regarding the prudence of his words: "But it would be impossible to make such statements, opinion in England would not stand it," etc. . . . As Sir Roderick reiterated his objections several times, Herr von Ribbentrop finally said, with a shade of irritation: "Don't you know that we don't care two pins for the reactions of public opinion either in our country or in others?"

It is most important that the handling of public opinion in France should be carefully regulated, in other words that the Commissariat of Information should have other powers and other capacities than those which Monsieur Daladier has given it.

FEBRUARY 15TH

France: a nation which thinks a great deal about the art of living.

Germany: a nation which thinks a great deal about the art of killing.

FEBRUARY 16TH

I took a few American visitors to see Monsieur
Dautry, Minister of Armaments. This little man, in-
defatigable in spite of his age—he is sixty—began
life by working very hard as an engineer of the State
Railroads; he first attracted attention during the
other war by performing a miracle: he built a hundred kilometers of railway in a hundred days in an
exposed section of the front. . . . With his lack of
eloquence—which distinguishes him so happily from
politicians—and his unstable but ardent glance,
Dautry gives the impression of complete honesty and
conviction. I do not know whether he is an organizer
but he is certainly a man who galvanizes others. What
he says about the cost of the war is food for much
thought. . . .

A 75 cannon costs 300,000 francs, the total equipment of an artillery regiment represents fifty million
francs; a battalion of heavy tanks is worth one hundred and twenty million francs. . . . A salvo from an
anti-aircraft cannon is four thousand francs gone up
in smoke; the bill for barrage firing on a front of one
kilometer for only five minutes comes to 300,000
francs. During an attack which lasts one hour a division spends five million francs in munitions. . . .

Such is the "standard of living" to which Germany

has finally condemned Europe and the world. When one thinks how much want, poverty and distress could have been relieved with the war budgets of the last five years, one despairs of human reason. However, we all but took the opposite direction, and the Disarmament Conference of 1932 was the last attempt at salvation. But Germany torpedoed the conference, although England (who has since bitterly regretted it) had already reduced her armaments. (We ourselves had reduced the length of military service to eighteen months, then to a year.) The race for rearmament began again and we entered the race, but too late to prevent Germany from provoking war. . . . For several years it has not been true in politics that "the worst is not always certain": this proverb needs to be revised.

FEBRUARY 18TH

Yesterday, met Paul Valéry again. For this great poet the war is a source of constant moral suffering. "The world is mad, we have known that for a long time," he murmured, "but now we have learned that it is mad with . . . stupidity."

FEBRUARY 20TH

"Well, do you think that your country is going to win the war, or not?" The American correspondent who asked this question was walking down the Rue de Rivoli with me; I saw, stuck up on a hoarding the celebrated poster: "We Are Going to Win Because we are the Strongest." I answered the question by pointing to the comforting poster, where one sees a map of the world and on this map, colored in pink, all the countries controlled by France and England; and the effect obtained is certainly a very bright and extensive splash of pink. . . . Later I asked myself once again the question put by my companion. When I say in the course of conversation that I believe victory is assured to us, I feel very keenly that I lack the enthusiasm to shout it out, but at the same time defeat is inconceivable to me, and doubtless a great many Frenchmen flounder in the same contradictions. . . . At present there is one sentence which is repeated everywhere; it is rather vague, but rather terrible, and it sums up the fluctuations of our thoughts: "We will win but we will have a *most difficult* summer."

It is curious to reflect that the facts which should furnish a clear, plain answer to the question: "Who will win the war?" should be known to us, but that other facts, thousands of secondary or deceptive facts, obstruct our brains: we are incapable of isolating the authentic elements from the others. A really clairvoyant mind would, like Joan of Arc before Charles the Seventh, the latter disguised in the midst of his courtiers, go straight to the unknown, saying: "This is the King." Which is the fact-king? What is the decisive fact of this war?

The poster "We Are Going to Win Because we are the Strongest," the work of one of Reynaud's departments, has been criticized to his face. He has been told: "You reason like the English; your map is very convincing indeed, *if* time is given to the French and British Empires to mobilize all these immense resources. And it is well known that some day the problem of iron and oil is going to become a critical one for the Third Reich, *but* not for some time. . . . Time is the unknown quantity of this equation. . . . For whom is time working?" Paul Reynaud threw his head back, a rather sardonic expression passed, as it often does, over his "Asiatic" face and he kept silence. At bottom he, too, often has moments of doubt, but at the same time one feels in him a sort of swaggering pluck, the conviction that matters will smooth out by themselves, particularly if he is called to take the helm. He gives two contradictory impressions: he is pitilessly lucid, he always sees the future of France in the darkest colors and, at the same time, he never appears to be discouraged for a single moment and he even goes on with his chaffing and bantering; he is simultaneously Cassandra and Gavroche the street urchin. I felt this strongly when I worked with him, four years before the war, on a little book entitled: *Young men, what kind of France do you want?* For those who were becoming more and more interested in politics, and who were trying to escape the old time-worn formulas and find something new, there were very few political men worthy of attention. . . . At the Chamber, Paul Reynaud appeared to be the man with the clearest, sharpest mind, the one whose speeches were the least distorted by professional politics. . . . This cold, precise orator did not mouth sonorous epithets, worthy, at best, of electoral meetings in the provinces. So it was quite appropriate to go and ask Paul Reynaud a certain number of questions and request him to develop them sufficiently for a small volume to be made of his answers.

Before lending this volume to a neutral journalist yesterday, I chanced to look over the pages and could not help being surprised to meet the contradictions I have just mentioned: "You are dying," Dr. Reynaud declared succinctly to the Republic, after listening to her heart and lungs—"but you'll pull through." His critical turn of mind and his gift for exact statements bring the author to define very clearly France's grave diseases, and he leads the reader to think that since the patient is at the point of death, medicine can do her no good and a surgeon should be resorted to. Now Reynaud limits himself to discussing reforms only, but these reforms are so considerable that they are indeed equal to a revolution. Naturally, in the light of present events, I see all this more clearly than I did a few years ago.

What keeps the demonstration from proceeding to its ultimate result is the fact that the author of the demonstration is a parliamentary man, an ambitious man who is thinking to himself: "Things would change completely if I were Prime Minister."

Another very energetic man belonging to the present regime, Georges Mandel, developed the same theory for me one day: "We lack leaders only. When a Prime Minister has enough vigor he remains in power, and the Chamber cannot prevent heads of government who are really leaders, from governing, etc. . . . " And Mandel, like Reynaud, named the rare ministries that lasted more than two years, those of Monsieur Clemenceau and Monsieur Poincaré, the regime's two last phenomena of longevity. Curiously enough, prolonged ministries are possible in France only when the country is skirting catastrophe: Monsieur Clemenceau remained in power because the war seemed all but lost when he was appointed Prime Minister; Monsieur Poincaré stayed in office long enough to revive the poor franc which was about to drown.

This question of institutions and of men is not so simple to solve as Reynaud and Mandel think. . . . It would be wrong to believe that a regime can be good in the absolute, but equally erroneous not to understand that when the legislative power has become excessive, as it has with us, the executive power has only the ghost of a chance to develop its authority.

At the time he compiled this little book, Reynaud lived in the Faubourg Saint Honoré and innumerable heads of Buddha seemed to listen there with perfect indifference to the discussions on French politics. . . . There were a great many books on the library shelves, because Reynaud read much, particularly in his youth, and on the walls there were also Japanese prints. The rapidity with which Reynaud throws an idea on paper, develops it and then polishes his text, is remarkable. His facility for work had also struck Lyautey, who worked even faster and whose hand, when he wrote, could never follow his thoughts rapidly enough. And then, after having finished a paragraph, Reynaud would call in one of his collaborators, one of those whom he called his "brain reserve" and ask his advice.

On military questions, several "brain reserves" helped him, notably Commandant de Gaulle. Questions I had asked Reynaud on this subject were very simple, coming as they did from one who possessed the average Frenchman's limited knowledge of these technical problems . . . well, he had found on his table a sheet of paper on which were pencilled several words, each word followed by a question mark: "Motorizing of the army?"—"Fortifications?"—etc. . . . Words which in 1936 had not yet kept us from sleep. The following passage from Reynaud's answer has seemed to me more curious than the others:

"A shock army" [1] of lightning speed and formidable firing power must be created. *Modern* armored tanks, ironclads of the land, have a speed of 40 kilometers an hour in open country. The firing capacity

---

[1] *Choc* means a rapid blow, something capable of colliding violently, or clashing.

of the specialized maneuvre corps—the creation of which I asked for in my counterproposal of March 31, 1935—would have been double that of the entire French Army of 1914. A hurricane sweeping everything before it.

"One still hears people talk of mass levies. Those who talk thus are old-fashioned. The mass levies were all very well when we had the mass. At the time of the Revolutionary Wars the population of France was as large as that of England and all the German Principalities put together.

"In a modern army, as in industry, man must be adapted to machinery. The great new factor of the next war will be explosive motive power.

"So let us play the trump card of quality. Let us play it boldly. What limits the power of a navy is not the number of men but the number of ships. What limits the power of an air force is the number of airplanes. What will, in the future, limit the power of ground forces will not be the number of men, it will be the number and power of its war machines.

"To have a military system which blocks our forces inside our frontiers would not only make us incapable of fulfilling our international obligations, it would not only mean that the collective security by which we hope to benefit in the day of peril, might be turned to the advantage of others, it would also mean committing a fundamental error of conception.

"Our organisations in the Northeast are very strong, but it would be an error to consider them positively insurmountable. We must not forget that

Russian, Belgian and French fortresses were taken during the last war without being destroyed, because of the mental shock suffered by garrisons subjected to the formidable ordeal of the siege. It appears likely that the German Army, preceded by powerful tanks for breaking down obstacles, will sweep over Holland into Belgium; there it is to be ardently hoped that the Albert Canal, which runs from Antwerp to Liége, will be strongly enough fortified and held to stop them. This failing, the German Army will take the direction of our northern frontier which is 350 kilometers wide.

"So it remains necessary, for our own national defence, that we should have a shock army capable of leaping to the help of the Belgian Army and victoriously repulsing that of the invaders, who would attempt a sudden aggression."

FEBRUARY 24TH

An English journalist describes in an article an airplane fight which took place by moonlight; he relates that at one moment he saw the Spitfire throwing itself in pursuit of the German plane, losing it, finding it once more and finally, he writes, "the English plane closed in on the enemy and machine-gunned it between Orion and the Pleiades." The British censor suppressed "between Orion and the

Pleiades," taking this to mean a topographical indication.

But our own censors are by no means inferior to their British colleagues. A provincial journalist wished, the other day, to publish an innocuous article on the prestige of certain foreign characters in French literature. "In the seventeenth century," he wrote, "the Castilian *caballero* served as a model for Corneille's *Cid*; in the eighteenth century the Englishman was made exaggeratedly fashionable by Voltaire, etc. . . ." The entire paragraph was suppressed by the censor as susceptible of creating difficulties for us with Spain and England.

What is less amusing is this: A debate about censorship and information has just taken place at the Chamber, a debate in which all the defects in the present system have been pointed out with admirable precision—but the speeches have not been followed by any results. This is typical and shows that the machinery is truly out of gear; everything for deliberation, nothing for execution. And that in spite of the war. Amid the unanimous applause of the assembly, it was proclaimed that the radio is cut into four parts, that the principal information escapes the Information, that there is no one in sole authority, that our telegrams and newspapers are always delayed in transmission and always defeated in foreign capitals in the battle of speed, that France has built a blockade around her own news, that in the United States, in December, 1939, out of a hundred lines devoted to foreign news, Germany received 31 as her share, England 22, Finland 13,

Russia 10, Italy 7, Japan 6, and France 5; that French photographs are supplanted by German photographs, etc. . . . "The authority of the government has defaulted," Monsieur Léon Blum declared in person.

For in this session the best argument was made by Monsieur Léon Blum. His speech said a great deal more than it appeared to say, and the orator, without being completely aware of it, did no more than plead at length for . . . the reinforcement of the executive power. That the leader of the opposition, the leader of the Socialist party and the man who goes further in parliamentary scruples than anyone else, should speak along the lines of the men who insist upon a reinforced State, is most significant. If one had not known who was speaking thus in the Chamber, one would never have guessed that it was the ex-Head of the Popular Front who was demanding: "Let the direction be what it will, it matters very little to me, but let there be a real direction." Or, when he talked about the radio: "One man, or simply a directorship, would be able to master this task, and without too much trouble." His theme, the needful concentration of authority, seems to obsess the speaker, and he does not mind repeating himself: "As to the propaganda-information-radio combination, it forms a necessarily indissoluble whole, it must be subjected to a single direction, inspiration and impulsion." And finally, the leader of the French Section of the Workers' International was heard to acknowledge, *en passant,* that Doctor

Goebbels' services were "organized with admirable and unexampled minuteness and perfection."

In short, at the left (Blum), in the center (Reynaud), and at the right of the Chamber are expressed isolated opinions which concur with what Tardieu wrote when he decided to leave the parliament. The diagnosis is the same in all quarters. How is it, then, that it is impossible to manage the repair of the machine and an increase in output? It is certainly not from ignorance of the cause of the evil. France abounds in clear-sighted minds which are continually furnishing her with admirable diagnoses, but as soon as a cure is attempted the situation changes.

The tragedy of our generation lies here: *Little by little, in our country, we have seen the idea of democracy completely divorced from the idea of efficiency.*

As a democracy without efficiency we are running towards ruin. And whither would we go but towards a disavowal of ourselves, having an efficiency which would condemn us to suppress certain democratic principles, principles absolutely indispensable to a complete flowering of French qualities?

Is this dilemma inevitable? In the last few years, every time certain orators have bluntly propounded political dilemmas ("Butter or cannons," "Authority or decadence," "Let us make Europe, or Germany will, etc. . . ."), numbers of us have protested with all our might. And now we cannot escape the conviction that certain brutal alternatives are forced upon us, that now we have only the choice between a life infinitely harder than any we have ever known, and death.

It is certain that we will not be able to vanquish Nazism if the war is continued in the present atmosphere, if we believe that we can keep conveniences and material luxury, and also de luxe liberties and de luxe ideas, during the conflict. There is no reason why democracy should not progress indefinitely, why it should not bring a citizen nearer and nearer to physical and mental well-being, nearer and nearer to a peace which would be the first condition of all these things *in a world where dictatorships did not exist*—just as there is no reason why you should not win if you play bridge well—but if one of your opponents cheats, then the game is no longer possible. It is then necessary for you also to cheat, and things are no longer as they were; you are dishonored or you throw the dishonest player out and then the game is interrupted: in both cases, *the game is no longer the same*. In our democratic countries, the game of institutions can no longer be the same either, since the Nazi adversary will not respect any of the rules of the game. . . . We have been loath to throw down our cards and punish the cheat, and we have thought the game could go on and that we could win (as we might have in former times) against an opponent who has marked his trumps. . . .

The pitiless fate of our generation will have been to recognize our obligation to make this unprecedented choice, and to have seen the leaders of our country elude the choice through lack of courage.

Certainly, if a few years ago we had placed our peacetime democracy on a war footing, as the *Comité de Salut Public*[1] in the French Revolution would have done to ward off danger, we would have had to suspend a few of our precious liberties and renounce many of the pleasures of life. And in acting thus, we surely would have run a risk, in spite of everything, the risk of never recovering some of what we had renounced. So much the worse, but that is a less serious risk than the other, and then, nothing ventured, nothing kept.

A great many Frenchmen have come to this conclusion slowly and much against their hearts. Others have a foreboding of the truth, but this truth has a most unpleasing face to look upon and they turn away. . . . It was to persuade certain Frenchmen to look certain distasteful facts in the face that *Jeunesse, quelle France veux-tu?* ("Young Men, what kind of France do you want?") appeared.

*
* *

In 1936 I attempted to crystallize French uneasiness in a few questions, and I asked Reynaud to furnish the replies. To mark the fact that the questioner was of small importance in the matter, "Curiosus" was my pseudonym; "Curiosus" was just any Frenchman questioning Reynaud about the problems of the day. . . . In 1940 Reynaud came into power and had the tragic fate of being Prime Minister during our defeat: well, it is very interesting to

[1] The "Committee of Public Safety" of the French Revolution.

observe that he prophetically described in "Young Men, what kind of France do you want?" *some of the causes of the final catastrophe. Hence the interesting quality of the following quotations, where Cassandra-Reynaud speaks without knowing that he is to be the chief actor in the tragedy foretold.*

Paul Reynaud: "Our task is to make a collective state of mind, necessary to the salvation of a threatened State, co-exist with individualism. France is the guardian of individualistic values. It is precisely because our formula of individualism is in danger that the vexed post-war doctrine of individual enjoyment must be rejected. It was a perversion of individualism. . . ."

"Curiosus": "Then to what task will you call the young men?"

Paul Reynaud: ". . . to the great problems which we must solve if we wish to survive. Europe is in peril in the world, France is in peril in Europe . . . no party has been able to make the necessary effort of renovation in the face of these new problems."

"Curiosus": "In short, you lay the blame on the middle classes, since the leaders of all parties are from the middle classes?"

Paul Reynaud: "In every class of society as in every political body there are partisans of immobility and partisans of movement. Alas, because of the small proportion of young men in politics the partisans of immobility are in the majority! They are afraid of thinking, in a country where thought has shone so brilliantly. And they fear its dynamism and build a barrier against all that does not conform with their static ideas. One might say that the French bourgeoisie which produced Voltaire, Condorcet, Lavoisier and many others, which took the lead in intellectual Europe, today appears to be vacillating and bewildered. It seems to follow at the end of the procession, in the world of today. The bourgeoisie goes outside of our frontiers to replenish its stock of political ideas. In the past, foreigners came to France to pillage ours. The bourgeoisie seems to be going to its doom, as did the nobility of the old regime in the wake of the Revolution. The nobility, at any rate, went smiling, while the bourgeoisie looks as though it were following its own funeral. . . ."

"Curiosus": "So there is, so to speak, insolvency on the part of the bourgeoisie before the present crisis of the regime?"

Paul Reynaud: "Yes. The parliamentary regime is *its* regime. Thanks to this regime, the bourgeoisie has been in power for the past century. And what do we find? Do the economic crisis and the peril from without demand that the State should have more rapid and more powerful reactions? Yes, but instead of struggling to save the regime by adapting it to present circumstances, the bourgeoisie does nothing but disparage it. Some even declare that the regime must be destroyed, without, however, daring to pronounce the words *coup d'état,* or taking the trouble to write down in black and white what they propose to put in its place. . . ."

"Curiosus": "You know the aspirations of young Frenchmen. You know that they long for political renovation. . . ."

Paul Reynaud: "It would be committing a fundamental error to believe that our youth could adopt as a permanent ideal marching by fours, like the German youth. Individualism is a trait of our civilisation. Individualism has produced the greatness of our civilization and has radiated it out into the world. The youth of our country has never tolerated the yoke of servitude and the police supervision that accompanies it. . . ."

"Curiosus": "However, you agree that political life, as we practise it, does not satisfy youth's desire to serve?"

Paul Reynaud: "Yes, I agree. But why is this? Because public life has been dragged down to the level of wretched personal matters, because youth is not provided with ideas, because it is not brought face to face with the great problems that have to be solved to stave off death. . . ."

"Curiosus": "But to accomplish these great tasks, should not the State first be reformed?"

Paul Reynaud: "I am of that opinion. . . . What is more, I do not believe in the magic virtues of regimes. We have tried them all. We can keep our balance only by preserving our ideal of liberty, even though we have to impose necessary disciplines upon ourselves."

"Curiosus": "So you believe that it would be better to modify the regime than to overturn it?"

Paul Reynaud: "Yes. . . ."

"Curiosus": "You think that the present regime could be adapted. On what points?"

Paul Reynaud: "First of all, I wish that the deputies no longer had the initiative in expenditures; for otherwise public finances will founder periodically. . . . Of course, the deputies can never be prevented from bringing pressure on the government to force it into demagogic expenditures. And here some fault must be found with electors who, in the abstract, demand good management of public finances, but who, in specific instances, are ready with the worst display of violence to oppose this good management. When a deputy votes some measure of economy, he perhaps attracts the tempered and passing gratitude of his electors but he provokes tenacious and vigilant hostility on the part of those electors who are affected by this measure. . . ."

"Curiosus": "What other electoral reforms would you wish?"

Paul Reynaud: "The Government should be given the right to dissolve the Chamber on its own authority. Thus the balance would be re-established between a legislative power which is too strong and an executive power which is too weak. . . . Also, dictatorial powers necessitated by either the economic crisis or the foreign crisis, in exceptional circumstances, would be applied by means of decree laws, thanks to the full powers conceded to the Government by the House. It was thus that the Roman Republic accorded full powers in times of stress and afterwards the regime resumed its normal course. . . ."

"Curiosus": "Could you also call the bourgeoisie insolvent in a crisis of security?"

Paul Reynaud: "Yes, the left parties are unanimous in wishing for collective security, but not in voting military credits. Men belonging to the right wing parties are unanimous in voting military credits but do not wish for collective security, without which comes isolation; that is a peril which military credits are not sufficient to guard against. As it is, the very conception of our army. . . ."

"Curiosus": "Would you say that the army plan or conception is inadequate?"

Paul Reynaud: "Late, at any rate, terribly behindhand. Do you think that the German Army would have occupied the left bank of the Rhine if we had had the mechanized shock army, whose creation I called for in a precise counterproposal a year ago? Herr Hitler knows that we have only a defensive army, slow to muster. We have kept to the army of 1927, conceived at the time when Stresemann's Germany knocked at the door of the League of Nations. . . ."

"Curiosus": "What objections were made to your counterproposal?"

Paul Reynaud: "I was answered: 'Don't hustle us. We must not confuse the army by making great changes.' And that, at a time where in other countries, in Germany and Russia, gigantic changes were boldly being undertaken! This misguided prudence has shown itself to be the direst imprudence."

"Curiosus": "Is France in a condition to play her part in the new organization of peace?"

Paul Reynaud: *"No, because she does not possess an instrument for her policy.* She has maintained the defensive army created by the law of 1927 which assigns to it a triple purpose, which is:

1. To insure the military training of Frenchmen.
2. To protect the territory of the mother country.
3. To insure the defence of overseas France.

As you see, this is a purely defensive army."

"Curiosus": "How could this situation be remedied?"

Paul Reynaud: "By the creation of a shock army, as I have already told you."

"Curiosus": "What would be the characteristics of this shock army, or specialized corps?"

Paul Reynaud: "It would be an implement of maneuvre, constantly in readiness, having steady power, gifted with great cohesion, able to use the swiftest war machines, and lastly, animated by the highest type of military spirit. The counterproposal which I laid before the rightful authorities in March, 1935 foresaw an effective force of a hundred thousand men, of which natives could form a fifth part. This corps would be composed of six infantry divisions and one light division, all of them motorized. . . ."

"Curiosus": "In other words, this would be a standing army?"

Paul Reynaud: "Yes, for reasons which hold good for the air force and, in a large measure, for the navy. If machinery requires specializing in industry, so much the more is this necessary in the army because of the unpredictable conditions under which those who handle it are called upon to utilize it. . . . This shock army would be the best of schools to form *cadres*. . . . What is more, the role of *cadres* would be more important than ever in a war where the combatants would operate in small groups, disposed on the terrain around collective weapons. . . ."

"Curiosus": "This plan for the creation of a professional army, a pretorian army, would, I should think, give rise to objections of a political nature. Isn't this so?"

Paul Reynaud: "The most democratic army is that which is best fitted to avoid a war."

"Curiosus": "The creation of this specialized maneuvre corps would involve considerable expense, would it not?"

Paul Reynaud: "As concerns war materiel, this expenditure has in every way been already calculated."

"Curiosus": "But, in spite of this, your plan has been discarded?"

Paul Reynaud: "Yes, in France. But it has been silently adopted in Germany."

"Curiosus": "Will we benefit by this lesson?"

Paul Reynaud: "Nothing allows me to think so for the time being. *We have an absurdly small number of modern tanks.* As for the four thousand old war tanks, they are inadequately armored. . . . When you add to this picture the fact that the new German 77 gun has a firing range of fourteen kilometers while our 75 gun has a range of ten or eleven kilometers, that the new German 105 has a range of seventeen kilometers and ours a range of thirteen and that the same differences in range exist in the heavy artillery, perhaps our young men will think with me that it is urgent to replace patriotic speeches

with cerebral efforts applied to our defence problem."

"Curiosus": "For that problem as well as for the
rest, you call for a change in the nation's state of
mind?"

Paul Reynaud: "Exactly."

MARCH 6TH

"A German plane came over Paris and traced a
circle of smoke, and another German plane flew over
the first one while it was tracing its mysterious sign."
This is what gossiping old wives are telling one another. And every one, to appear well-informed, tells
a story about the King of England: his intentions,
they say, were so well guessed-at by the enemy when
he visited the front that the German radio announced ahead of time each of the places which the
sovereign had decided to see. It is evident that one
of the observations by which German propaganda
benefits most is this: "No one can resist the desire
of being the first to spread a picturesque story." So
the next move is to invent certain anecdotes, or, taking a true detail as a starting point, to build up an
amusing fable; after which, success is assured. In a
country where conversation is as much liked as it is
in France, millions of talkers innocently turn them-

selves into sowers of German propaganda, and at the office, in cafés, in garages, at lunch or at dinner, will repeat any little story capable of attracting notice.

In studying the laws of psychology which determine whether or not one takes interest in this thing or that, excellent propaganda recipes must surely be found; and this is what the Germans have done. They have delved deeply into the matter, treating it like a new science; and in Germany there even are institutions where this strange science is taught, like chemistry or mechanics.

Nazi agents have added a new invention to the already lengthy list of their creations: the "personal" visit to a home. A "school friend" of a mobilized man goes to see the wife of the absent soldier and expresses a banal sympathy for his old friend. But this so-called comrade notices every detail of the apartment which he visits. And after this visit a letter is sent to the mobilized man, where he is told all about the "scandalous life" led by his wife during his absence, "because of this filthy war," and authentic details of the apartment give a certain air of truth to this mendacious report. . . . The new German leaflet thrown over Paris: "Frenchmen, Prepare Your Coffins" has provoked a good many remarks. There is also the "red notebook," a little pamphlet printed on apparently exquisite paper which furnishes the French populace with statistics proving the certainty of Hitler's victory. Many examples of leaflets have passed before our eyes; at the end of last year we had a specimen which might be called the "poetical leaflet." Imagine a sheet of paper shaped like a leaf and rust-colored, on which some kind German has written that the trees will bear new leaves in the spring but French soldiers who fall for the British cause will never live again, etc. . . . One might wonder whether these leaflets raining down on our front lines would not produce a depressing effect there, but reassuring news came quickly. The soldiers, for the most part peasants, said: "Don't understand." For once the specialists across the Rhine who had this esthetic idea missed their mark. The composition of a song (anti-British) which recently came down from heaven and was purported to be sung by Maurice Chevalier, had a surer effect. Another German idea was to print a false *Paris-Soir,* called *Paris-Noir.* Well in evidence beside the title *Paris-Noir* could be read the following doggerel:

	(translation)
Paris d'antan, ta gloire	*Paris of yesteryear, your glory*
Etait ta lumière	*Was your bright lighting*
Paris maintenant Paris-Noir	*Paris now dark Paris*
Pourquoi la guerre?	*Why this war?*

This French might be that of an anti-military negro poet. On the other side of the title Stuttgart's refrain was printed: "England will fight to the last Frenchman." Ferdonnet and Obrecht, star traitors on the Stuttgart scene, have been condemned to death *absente reo.*

MARCH 7TH

General Mason MacFarlane has attended one of our last Anglo-French committee meetings. He does not speak much, and seems clever. He has been in Germany as military attaché and knows the Germans very well. Somebody asks him who is the most dangerous German general.

"Our worst enemy," says he, "is General Wishful Thinking."

MARCH 8TH

Still the coffee question. Fourteen thousand tons are in customs, or we might say, in sufferance; this has been announced in great haste to the French, putting an end to their sufferings also. On the other hand, from the 18th of March on, there will be three meatless days a week, after which it is hinted that we may have a bread card and two or three days out of seven when the sale of pastry will be prohibited. Here is a curious fact: the more privations introduced, the fewer recriminations one hears. This is a psychological law, well-known to all, but of which deputies are ignorant: if people have a right to one piece of sugar in their *café au lait* instead of the traditional two, they are ready to riot, but if they are threatened with the suppression of the entire breakfast, they understand that things are serious and feel rather proud of such importance. The concierge of the house next to mine grew so excited on reading the list of restrictions he found a nickname for Paul Reynaud: "Just look what he's treating us to, Popaul Decree law!" However, he was wrong in attributing all these mortifications to Reynaud, who is not responsible for them. But as the Minister of Finance before the war imposed fresh taxes, and has since preached a good deal about a general tightening of belts, he is held responsible for all the punishments meted out to France; he is our national bogeyman. From this dread he enjoys a sort of highly peculiar, inverted popularity.

In short, our standard of living, which remains superior to that of the Germans, nevertheless continues to decline, just as does their own. Just as bad money chases away genuine money, so a bad table chases away a good table. From a certain angle this war seems to be caused by the jealousy of one neighbor for another neighbor: those who eat herrings and sausages have sworn that those in the garden across the way who are delicately dissecting a fat cutlet shall end too by settling down to a Spartan regime of bricks. . . .

Frenchmen have never grumbled over work when matters are serious, and Paul Morand was right when he declared one day that the French vice was work. One has only to know the tenacity of labor in our peasants to be convinced of this. "A Frenchman is like a thoroughbred, walk him and he will go to sleep," General Bonnel once remarked. This is a truth that has been forgotten. But has the thoroughbred been awakened in time?

MARCH 9TH

An article has appeared in Switzerland saying that the French system of fortifications between the Ardennes and the North Sea is much less solid than was thought. The High Command has again sent us a refutation:

"At the beginning of the war there was only one Maginot Line. Now there are two. The first one took up 12 million cubic yards of ground, and 1,500,000 cubic yards of reinforced concrete were used on it. It took six years to build it. The second line was built in three months.

"Naturally the second Maginot Line is less imposing than the first, but it is supplemented by reinforced lines of resistance which stretch from the Forest of Ardennes to the North Sea and from the foot of the Jura Mountains to the Swiss frontier. Four million five hundred thousand cubic yards of earth have been used during the three months that it has taken to build this new line. If these earth-works had been constructed with a view to making a canal of normal width, this canal would already be nearly 120 miles long.

"The volume of reinforced concrete used comes to 700,000 cubic yards and this would represent a wall one yard high, one yard broad and 450 miles long.

"Since the beginning of September our soldiers have laid down 16,500,000 square yards of barbed wire entanglements. This covers a space which, if it were four yards wide, would reach half way from the Pole to the Equator, that is 2,400 miles. Four million stakes have been used to wedge in these entanglements.

"What is more, the trenches, armored pill boxes and barbed wire are but a part of the battlefield equipment.

"Our armies have been employed in thousands of other occupations. Keeping the roads in condition alone is an incredible task. In spite of the enormous lorries which have been on the move continually since the first day of mobilization, these roads still are in excellent condition, thanks to the care which they have been given. Means of transportation in modern warfare is of primary importance, and the large number and fine quality of French highways have proved to be of inestimable advantage.

"The fact that the operations outlined here have been pursued without a break since the beginning of hostilities shows the abundance of our economic resources.

"In Germany, on the contrary, the government has met with great difficulties. The questioning of prisoners of war has revealed that the enemy's construction work has been halted several times from lack of material, particularly of iron.

"In three months our chances of breaking any enemy offensive have been tremendously increased. We have won with machinery and saved the blood of our country while obtaining a great defensive victory.

"It is easy to understand why in the 'Order of the Day' of December 25th, General Gamelin mentioned the 'immense fortifications completed.' The French Army has not wasted its time."

MARCH 13TH

Heredity and the Racial Theory, a little book by Jean Rostand which has just appeared, establishes without long and useless argument that "racial theories are gratuitous structures founded on a puerile and biassed anthropology." Rostand recalls that some of the highest manifestations of human genius were the work of composite races. His opposition to racial theories, however, is accompanied by high praise of eugenics, and his judgments constantly show a freedom of mind most agreeable to find . . . in war time. But this book also has an effect of dreariness, for Rostand's keen intelligence envisages the gloomiest prospects.

What one principally retains, on putting down this small volume, is the impression that civilization is but a limited, artificial and most precarious thing. It would seem that in becoming better, man becomes weaker, and the most cultured peoples are those that are most closely threatened with disappearance. This recalls the history of the mountain and plain tribes of India: at a period when the plain tribes begin to perfect their architecture, dress, music, customs, etc., men from the mountains invariably and regularly swooped down and exterminated those who, by becoming superior to them mentally, were now their inferiors, muscularly speaking. . . . I remember a football coach at the Paris University Club, who was furious at not receiving marks of consideration from certain students of the "intellectual clan" and exclaimed: "If I were to assemble my team and if we were to rush for the library at the Sorbonne, ah! I know who would get a licking: in five minutes all those spectacled guys who sit over books all day would be torn to pieces by my boys!" And he certainly would have been the victor. . . .

The facts which Rostand brings to light in refutation of the racial theories are known to everyone in every country, and so the ideas which the Nazis teach children in their schools must, in spite of scientific appearances, be a tissue of lies, purposely imposed upon young brains. We have had rather comical echoes of the perplexity of certain German students, to say nothing of the educators. By dint of lyrically vaunting the blond, dolichocephalic northern type, representing the purest element of the Aryan race, school teachers finally created an inferiority complex among the brown haired children; and statistics pitilessly revealed that dark hair, complexion and eyes widely predominated in Southern Germany. Blonds existed in the proportion of 40 percent—the maximum figure—only in certain eastern regions.

And on the other hand, educators were extremely embarrassed when some of their scholars—far too cunning for their taste—asked why it was, if Germans belonged to one race only, that certain among them were fair, others dark, some had the long dolichocephalic skull, others the round brachycephalic skull. . . .

MARCH 18TH

The peace signed between Russia and Finland made a bad impression on the public, who felt that it had been fooled; at the Chamber this reaction showed itself in a fashion most dangerous for the cabinet. The secret session in the Senate was stormy, and a rehandling of the Ministry was discussed immediately afterwards. As the Hitler-Mussolini meeting on the Brenner boded no good, discouragement and uneasiness are very keen at present. If at the end of the Senate's secret session Monsieur Daladier obtained a vote of confidence amounting to two hundred and thirty-six, it means that the Assembly does not wish to seem too brutal, but sixty of its representatives abstained from voting. Briefly, the War Government of France is in a bad way, and in spite of censorship a newspaper succeeded in publishing, apparently by chance, a little article evoking and regretting our Clemenceau of 1917.

Monsieur Daladier had already been displeased at the Chamber some time ago at being given a unanimous vote, for when an assembly shows mass approval, it does not vote for a ministry but merely in the interests of France. No one unfamiliar with parliamentary finesses could understand this mode of procedure. The Chamber now uses another weapon: abstention, for by reason of the war, open opposition is not resorted to. . . .

Daladier says in his own defence that the resolution to help Finland had been taken weeks ago, the creation of an expeditionary force had been decided on February 5th and two obstacles afterwards barred the way: The Scandinavian countries refused to allow French troops to pass, in spite of a letter written to King Gustavus of Sweden by the French Prime Minister; and Finland, in the last weeks of the war, did not call for our help. The censorship refuses to allow the publication of an article in which Mr. Hore-Belisha says practically the same thing in the following terms: "An expeditionary corps had been prepared and all necessary means taken to send it to Finland. Ships were ready in the ports, the engines under steam. Why did this army never sail? A complete explanation has not yet been given. It is known, however, that the Norwegian and Swedish governments threatened to oppose the transit of this army over their territories.

"The governments of Great Britain and France were apparently disposed to brave this opposition if the Finnish government had sent them a new appeal for help. The call did not come and a Punic peace was signed instead."

The British ex-minister said that the expeditionary force should have obtained right of passage across the Scandinavian countries as the latter belonged to the League of Nations, for the League of Nations had protested against the aggression. As always, according to right and equity, we hold trump cards. But in view of the facts, what? This is what happened in reality, as Mr. Hore-Belisha discovered after many others had done so: "The terror provoked by Russia and Germany influences the policies of the neutral European states more and more. . . ." And he concludes: "The Allies should improve their diplomacy and uphold it by acts."

Yes, the whole world shamefully gives way to fear, but there is a remark which no one has openly made except Cardinal Verdier; this remark is extremely apt. He said at the beginning of the war: "Formerly the world was not so frightened, and it used to protest against gangsters far less high-flown than those of today. The Germany of Wilhelm the Second, which was guilty of far less brigandage than Hitler's and which still submitted to certain Christian laws, this Imperial Germany had drawn upon itself the active execration of almost all the civilized world. One cannot say as much of the Germany which flies the swastika banner."

Since the "progress" of aviation, the powers of destruction doubtless inspire a far greater terror than formerly, and virtue, with the powers of indignation which she represents, has greatly decreased in the world during recent years. How many times have we heard people who would not harm a fly, give way, in spite of everything, before the creed of force, and murmur, in talking of *him:* "All the same, how strong he is!" I remember what happened to a friend who went to a Hitlerian meeting, in Berlin, a few years ago. He was more than surprised when one of those at the meeting, hearing him speak French, leaned forward after Hitler's speech and said to him, in French: "La raison du plus fort est toujours la meilleure." [1] The moral of the fable about the wolf and the lamb, which this stranger thought would be amusing to quote to a foreigner, secretly dwells within many minds which would not admit frankly that they approved of the wolf and thought his exploits admirable. This is a painful but unquestionable fact.

We must—and perhaps this necessity is among the cruelest that are forced upon us—recover a certain brutality to fight as we should against Hitler, but at the same time this momentary violence must not alter the essential part of our natures—for it would still be a defeat if, after defeating Hitlerism, we

[1] The reason of the strongest is always the best.

should keep the least taint of the brutality we were forced to adopt.

MARCH 21ST

Monsieur Daladier was told that he should not go before the Chamber without first reshuffling his Ministry, that the Senate's vote allowed him to change or reduce his staff of ministers and that, after having refurbished this staff, he would obtain certain success at the Palais-Bourbon. But he would not listen to the advice of experts in parliamentary strategy and he came before the secret committee in a reduced state and made a very tame speech; after which only 239 deputies voted for him, while 300 abstained from voting. After this result, which was disastrous to his prestige, the Prime Minister could do only one thing, resign. He seemed somewhat relieved—but at the same time, ambition for power will recapture him now that he has lost it. Then again, following the selfish advice of his friends, he will promptly be induced to lay traps along the path of his successor.

Daladier's case is most peculiar. It is the case of a man whom destiny has offered great opportunities (February 6, 1934, November 30, 1938, September 3, 1939) and who has not known how to profit by them. When an insurrection threatened Paris in

1934, he . . . turned over the pages of the legal code
to find out whether or not some law authorised him
to take certain measures. The Minister of the Interior at that time asked the Prime Minister to come
out openly on one side or the other; Daladier did
not reply but remained deeply immersed in his reading of the code. This little scene shows at once the
scruples of a professor at the height of power and his
inability to turn himself into a man of action when
the critical hour has struck. . . . After the General
Strike of November, 1938, and after his triumphal
tour in North Africa, Daladier had public opinion
behind him but he did not know how to use this immense advantage; and once more he missed the boat
when, on the declaration of war, the Parliament and
the public gave him a free hand.

In peace time a cabinet crisis alarms but a few
thousand persons, and that is why deputies risk very
little in throwing down ministries like so many ninepins; but in war time, it is another matter. A civilian
is not much interested in the governing powers in
peace time, but once he has become a soldier, he
likes to be commanded: then anything that proves
the weakness of the executive power brings a corresponding slump in the army morale.

*
*   *

*Here is the incredibly long list of our cabinets;
this list says more concerning the weak point of our
form of democracy than all the reports in the world:*

September 4, 1870: Gambetta...	5 months, 14 days
February 19, 1871: Dufaure....	2 years, 3 months
May 18, 1873: Dufaure........	7 days
May 25, 1873: de Broglie.......	6 months
November 26, 1873: de Broglie..	6 months
May 22, 1874: de Cissey........	10 months
March 10, 1875: Buffet........	11 months
February 23, 1876: Dufaure....	15 days
March 9, 1876: Dufaure........	9 months
December 12, 1876: Jules Simon	5 months
May 17, 1877: de Broglie......	6 months
November 23, 1877: de Roche-bouet	20 days
December 13, 1877: Dufaure....	1 year, 2 months
February 4, 1879: Waddington..	10 months
December 28, 1879: de Freycinet	9 months
September 23, 1880: Jules Ferry	1 year, 2 months
November 14, 1881: Gambetta...	2 months, 15 days
January 30, 1882: de Freycinet..	7 months
August 7, 1882: Duclerc........	6 months
January 29, 1883: Fallières....	28 days
February 26, 1883: Jules Ferry..	2 years, 2 months
April 6, 1885: Henri Brisson....	9 months
January 7, 1886: de Freycinet..	11 months
December 11, 1886: René Goblet	5 months, 17 days
May 30, 1887: Rouvier........	7 months
December 12, 1887: Tirard....	4 months
April 3, 1888: Charles Floquet..	10 months
February 22, 1889: Tirard.....	13 months
March 17, 1890: de Freycinet...	1 year, 11 months
February 27, 1892: Loubet.....	9 months
December 6, 1892: Ribot......	1 month
January 11, 1893: Ribot.......	3 months
April 4, 1893: Charles Dupuy..	8 months
December 3, 1893: Casimir Périer	5 months, 27 days
May 30, 1894: Charles Dupuy..	1 month
July 1, 1894: Charles Dupuy....	6 months, 25 days

January 26, 1895: Ribot....... 9 months
November 1, 1895: Leon Bour-
    geois .... 6 months
April 29, 1896: Méline........ 2 years, 2 months
June 28, 1898: Henri Brisson... 4 months
November 1, 1898: Charles
    Dupuy .... 4 months
February 18, 1898: Charles
    Dupuy .... 4 months
June 22, 1898: Waldeck-Rous-
    seau .... 3 years
June 7, 1902: Combes.......... 2 years, 7 months
January 24, 1905: Rouvier..... 1 year, 1 month
February 18, 1906: Rouvier.... 3 weeks
March 14, 1906: Sarrien....... 7 months
October 25, 1906: Clemenceau.. 2 years, 9 months
July 24, 1909: Briand........ 1 year, 4 months
November 3, 1910: Briand..... 4 months
March 2, 1911: Monis.......... 4 months
June 27, 1911: Caillaux....... 7 months
January 14, 1912: Poincaré.... 1 year
January 21, 1913: Briand...... 1 month
February 18, 1913: Briand...... 1 month
March 22, 1913: Barthou...... 9 months
December 9, 1913: Doumergue.. 6 months
June 9, 1914: Ribot........... 5 days
June 13, 1914: Viviani........ 2 months, 15 days
August 26, 1914: Viviani...... 1 year, 2 months
October 29, 1915: Briand...... 1 year, 2 months
December 12, 1916: Briand.... 3 months
March 20, 1917: Ribot........ 6 months
September 12, 1917: Painlevé.. 2 months
November 16, 1917: Clemenceau 2 years, 2 months
January 20, 1920: Millcrand.... 1 month
February 18, 1920: Millerand.. 7 months
September 24, 1920: Leygues... 4 months
January 16, 1921: Briand...... 1 year

January 15, 1922: Poincaré....	2 years, 2 months
March 29, 1924: Poincaré......	2 months, 15 days
June 9, 1924: François Marsal..	5 days
June 14, 1924: Herriot........	10 months
April 17, 1925: Painlevé.......	6 months
October 29, 1925: Painlevé....	1 month
November 28, 1925: Briand....	4 months
March 9, 1926: Briand........	3 months, 14 days
June 23, 1926: Briand........	26 days
July 19, 1926: Herriot........	4 days
July 23, 1926: Poincaré.......	2 years, 4 months
November 11, 1928: Poincaré...	8 months, 15 days
July 29, 1929: Briand........	3 months, 5 days
November 3, 1929: Tardieu....	3 months, 15 days
February 21, 1930: Chautemps..	10 days
March 2, 1930: Tardieu........	9 months
December 13, 1930: Steeg......	1 month, 15 days
January 27, 1931: Laval........	1 year
January 13, 1932: Laval........	1 month
February 20, 1932: Tardieu....	4 months
June 3, 1932: Herriot..........	6 months, 15 days
December 19, 1932: Paul-Boncour	1 month, 15 days
January 31, 1933: Daladier.....	9 months
October 26, 1933: Sarraut......	1 month
November 27, 1933: Chautemps	2 months
January 31, 1934: Daladier.....	9 days
February 9, 1934: Doumergue..	9 months
November 9, 1934: Flandin....	6 months, 22 days
May 31, 1935: Bouisson........	8 days
June 8, 1935: Laval...........	7 months, 16 days
January 24, 1936: Sarraut......	4 months, 10 days
June 4, 1936: Blum............	1 year, 18 days
June 22, 1937: Chautemps.....	6 months, 26 days
January 18, 1938: Chautemps...	1 month, 24 days
March 13, 1938: Blum.........	28 days
April 11, 1938: Daladier.......	1 year, 4 months, 23 days

September 4, 1939: Daladier. . . .   6 months, 17 days
March 21, 1940: Reynaud. . . . . .   ?

*

*   *

This extraordinary frequency of cabinet changes is strictly peculiar to us, and an executive power in a state of perpetual unsteadiness is not seen in other democracies—in the British democracy, for instance. Monsieur de Fleuriau, French Ambassador to London, explained one day to King George the Fifth why cabinets were so frequently changed in France: "I see," said the king, "it means, in short, that it is a feat for one of your deputies *not* to become a minister. . . ."

A magazine recently recalled that from 1895 to the war, England had had nine prime ministers only, while in the same interval we had had thirty-three, with seventy different cabinets. In the sixteen years which preceded the war, there were but three names in England: Baldwin and MacDonald, who alternated several times, and Chamberlain; whereas, in our country, seventeen different names governed in turn, with thirty-six "teams"! It has been figured that the average life of a French ministry was seven months. Sixteen of these ministries lasted less than three months, and seven fell on the very day they made their bow before the chamber. During the last ten years the frequency of these cabinet crises has surpassed anything seen up to that period, and President Lebrun has called more new prime ministers to take the helm than any other chief of state since the Republic was proclaimed. The reason for this is that internal peril (finances) and external peril have never been more serious; in this storm men have been knocked down like ninepins.

With scarcely a day's interval between them, Daladier came into power in France and Hitler in Germany. But while the Führer remained in his place, sixteen French ministries succeeded one another. In short, on one side a single government ordered guns, while on the other side sixteen ephemeral sets of men followed each other, and these men were far more preoccupied by the butter question than by the gun question. For in the immense majority of cases our governments fell on account of economic or financial quarrels. After having spent money unwisely and at random, the state exchequer had to be replenished and taxpayers burdened afresh, and this is where all the heads of government tripped and fell. It would be necessary from time to time to increase taxes—and discontent, and the discontented ended sooner or later by having their revenge.

The stereotyped phrase, "France, at a critical moment always finds the pilot who saves her" so complacently repeated because it is so comforting, has proved itself in recent years extremely debatable. The political men of today seem decidedly inferior to those of yesterday. Clemenceau and Poincaré seem giants compared with their successors. Why this decadence in politics when no such decadence exists in letters or science?

The appointment of Reynaud to the office of prime minister has given birth to hope in certain circles. He has taken pains to show himself, in latter years, as a man who belonged neither to the right nor to the left, but as one who wished to make a synthesis of all that was good in the right and the left. When there was a question of finding a good sentence for the band of paper [1] which was going to be slipped around *Young Men, What Kind of France Do You Want?* Reynaud pushed away the samples which were shown him and chose this: "Right? Left? No. Something new." A formula which summed up his ideas very well.

In France youth counts less than anywhere else. The consequences of the decrease in our birth rate are cruelly felt, and in no way more cruelly than in this: men over forty are relatively more numerous in France than in other countries. (And, to state a fact, there are three young Frenchmen twenty to thirty years old for four Englishmen, four Italians, seven Germans and fifteen Russians.)

The older set, on the other hand, has perfected a remarkable organization which allows it to close all means of access to newcomers—and to new plans—in the army as well as in politics. In refusing to bring youth into its life, our democracy has condemned itself to extreme conformity in most domains, and in all matters has erected the principle of *status quo* into a sort of dogma.

Now there are to be found, in the youth of France, extraordinary resources of enthusiasm and inventiveness, which, mobilized in the service of democracy, would have restored its lost dynamic powers.

[1] This corresponds to the jackets of books, in America.

One of the bitterest ordeals of our generation will have been to see the forces of the future harnessed to an evil cause by the "gentlemen across the way." [1] In this arrangement the Germans have invented nothing, they have merely copied what other revolutions —and notably ours—had already done. Thus they are ahead of us, for a younger staff of workers finds new techniques in all branches and moves more rapidly with its times than its elders can. In his *History of the French Revolution,* Thiers, in this case a most impartial observer, declares that one of the reasons for the unexpected French victories was that new tactics and new methods were created by revolutionaries who introduced new ideas everywhere they went, into everything they touched. (Napoleon was merely this spirit of innovation incarnated in a leader with genius, and that is why Austria always lagged behind him; as someone has said, she was late by one idea, one year and one army.)

Reynaud, especially in the question of military problems, has posed during recent years as the champion of innovations, and that is why some young men turn to him today. But the fact that he has had to gaze at the world for long years through the windows of Parliament has necessarily distorted his outlook. And will this distortion be stronger than his audacity? And how much can audacity do, when it is restricted by the "working" conditions imposed by legislators upon the executive power? How much can executive power do? That is what we shall see.

[1] "Ces messieurs d'en-face." Expression used by the soldiers to designate the Germans.

MARCH 22D

I went to the Ministry of Finances where affluence —the affluence of candidate ministers around Reynaud, was very great. The President of the Republic has asked Reynaud to form a new cabinet, and Monsieur Lebrun's choice is a natural one. The outgoing Prime Minister has shown himself to be a weak man, and so it is logical to call in a successor who passes for a "strong man." Reynaud said to me: "I come too soon, the situation is not ripe." Which means that he had hoped to be Prime Minister, but only after Daladier had been even further discredited. If a transition ministry, one of the queer, pale ministries we so often see, had succeeded Daladier, then Reynaud could have come to power with every chance of success. . . . All such Oriental subtleties have nothing to do with the reality of present problems, and it is astonishing that they can survive in war time. Indeed, there are as many visits, as many comings and goings and automobiles and telephone calls (telephone calls from fair intriguers) in the Rue de Rivoli building as there would be during a peacetime cabinet crisis. And the usual *laisser aller*, an incredible milling throng in the huge, gloomy antechamber of the Louvre. Under the old regime herds of courtiers used to leave the dying king's apartment to hurl themselves at the dauphin's door; and today, in the same manner, friends of Daladier could be seen knocking at the door of the dauphin of the day. In the old days, the beauty of costumes at least made this a sight agreeable to the eye, but such is not the case now. Ushers were pushing as best they could through the grayish mass of ministerial candidates; the latter talked in low tones, without ceasing to watch the visitors who lifted the great faded curtain which masks the entrance to Reynaud's office. Our democracy has no taste for the appropriate setting; this struck me today as much as it did a few years ago at Versailles when Doumer was elected to the Presidency of the Republic. This is very much to be regretted for the sake of the Republic, and no remedy has been found for this lack of suitable staging; the person of the chief of state (or of a government member) produces no "effect" whatsoever.

Reynaud had not slept a wink last night; his face was drawn and he asked himself whether fortune, after having smiled upon him, was not about to turn her back. For political confusion is at its height. Since the Socialists have agreed, by eighty votes against seven, and with numerous abstentions, to participate in the Cabinet, it is evident that Reynaud as Prime Minister is not so favorably viewed by the left wing as was thought. To rally his party colleagues, Blum has been obliged to say, "It is false to think that Reynaud has any intention of deciding an offensive." As Blum multiplied his exhortations in the lobbies, the right wing immediately spread the report that the entire cabinet crisis had been engineered by Reynaud and Blum, and decided not to give its cooperation to the budding ministry. This is what we have come to: the head of a government, considered rightly or wrongly as our "strongest" man, that is, the most capable of directing the war to victory with rapidity and energy, finds the Nationalist party against him.

The list of ministers is made haphazardly: according to the arithmetical combination which is permitted, so as to make a majority, one name or another is jotted down on the list of posts to be filled. Many a minister has thus been "oriented" by chance, in one direction or the other, at the beginning of his career; Campinchi tells readily, for instance, that the first time he was offered a post, it was the Ministry of Colonies; he was about to accept it when, a minute later, he was given the Ministry of the Navy.

Reynaud's collaborators have not concealed their disappointment, nor the disappointment which they believe will be the public's, over a final list of twenty-two ministers and thirteen under-secretaries of state. Rarely have so many colorless politicians been seen rowing in the same galley, and the mediocrity of the crew would have provoked little surprise had not the captain been announcing for years that he would recruit his collaborators in a most original manner, that is, solely according to their spirit of enterprise and their qualities as men of action. What has become of the famous elasticity of our institutions, so often celebrated by Poincaré in the past? The regime seems to have become incapable of adapting itself to circumstances, and its one idea, once the catastrophe has come, is to form a cabinet of national unity or to grant full powers to the government. There have been national unity cabinets after internal crises but it is curious to note that external peril has not been able to create a single one, even during the war. As to the full powers, those who have used them do not seem to have achieved very much with them. . . .

Reynaud's idea in making up his lamentable list is no doubt to avoid frightening the House, but what is the advantage of this, if an intelligent man finds himself condemned to as much mediocrity as any other man? And also if he belongs to no party and he is reduced to currying favor from one and all.

And therein lies Reynaud's weakness: he is alone. And he cannot truthfully say that he has the country behind him, for the mass of Frenchmen know little about him: the Chamber is aware of this and looks rather condescendingly upon the disarmed Minister.

Because of this situation, Reynaud has been forced to silence his real feelings and ask Daladier to become part of the Cabinet as Minister of War. Daladier accepted because his friends told him, after some political "soundings," that Reynaud would have a short ministerial life: so it would be better that Daladier should not refuse his co-operation; if he did, the Cabinet would fall on the spot, and this might seem like personal vengeance. Whereas, by supporting Reynaud, or by feigning to do so, Daladier's attitude would be a more elegant one, etc. . . .

An officer from a Maginot Line sector visited by

Reynaud this winter told me some weeks ago that the Minister had not made a very favorable impression upon the soldiers. "Why?"—"Because he went to see them in a fine derby hat and elegant pelisse; the men prefer Daladier, his old soft hat, shabby raincoat, cigarette hanging from his lip and his Marseille shopkeeper accent. . . ." Today the derby hat finds that it can do nothing without the collaboration of the soft hat. . . .

However, though Reynaud took Daladier into his cabinet, he refused to give Daladier's political protégé, Guy La Chambre, the post of Aviation Minister which the latter had held. During the secret session questions were asked concerning the deplorable state of our aviation, and the ex-minister saved his face, it is said, by quoting false figures. The chief editor of the *Petit Parisien* implored Reynaud to leave Guy La Chambre in office, but Reynaud refused, at the risk of alienating the said newspaper. So if, on the whole, Reynaud has lacked boldness in cooking the ministerial dish according to the oldest recipes, he still is capable of courage under special circumstances.

What seems surprising is the fact that since his ex-Chief of Staff, Palewski, has been removed, Reynaud has had no one to act as confidante in the lobbies of the Chamber. This confidential person, whose task is eavesdropping, persuading, hinting and whispering and being in all ways a valuable canvasser for his minister, does not seem to be missed by Reynaud. That is to say, he does not thoroughly exploit his political profession, while at the same time he does sacrifice himself to certain rules of the parliamentary game; he is a politician and he is not; his character is most complex. I think that a very strong belief in his guiding star explains these indiscretions: he walks about unarmed in enemy country for he thinks that his adversaries will not dare kill him.

When he was asked what was to be said to the foreign correspondents, he replied with a smile: "Tell them that I'm a heretic." He undoubtedly feels a secret pleasure in being so often right—against a majority—and this feeling includes a good deal of pride.

Furthermore, it would appear that this satisfaction is shared by very diverse minds in France. The reason is that, having attempted to modify the course of politics and not having succeeded, they seek in criticism the satisfaction they did not find in action. Reynaud, in the course of his earlier experiences as minister, sought to bring about great reforms but was not successful; for instance, in 1934 he was on the point of obtaining from Doumergue a change in the constitution, etc. . . . but failed.

After I had read to the American journalists a biographical note about Reynaud which they had asked for, I was struck by several facts which I had not sufficiently noticed before.

First of all, there is no longer anything about Reynaud which recalls his peasant origin. Born on the rugged plateaus of the Alps, he was sent to Paris— early, it is true—to pursue his studies. Some of his family, like many others from the Basses-Alpes Department, had emigrated to Mexico, there to grow rich through trading; so they were able to gratify the dream of every provincial: to send the youngster to Paris. And, as he was not born on the banks of the Seine, Reynaud wished all the more to pass for a Parisian. He often used to say: "I was born at Barcelonette, by chance."

After the Bossuet school and the Lycée Louis-le-Grand, the Parisian by adoption did what very few French bourgeois have the opportunity or desire to do: he made a tour around the world. On his return he became a lawyer, and was Secretary for the Lawyers' Conference. Then he treated himself to a pleasure which he frequently indulged in later: he caused a scandal in the temple of respectability: as Secretary of the Conference he had the privilege of making a speech before all his colleagues, and he chose to speak about Waldeck-Rousseau, a politician who was considered at that time to hold very advanced ideas! It took the personal authority of the President of the Bar Association to persuade the bold secretary to drop this dangerous subject and discuss instead the trial of King Charles the First of England. Elected deputy from Barcelonette in 1919, Reynaud surprised and disconcerted his colleagues, who also were much smitten with tradition: so much so that he was not re-elected. In 1926 he tried unsuccessfully to win against a Communist candidate, was defeated and did not return to the Chamber until 1928. Once more he takes unwonted initiatives; as Minister of Finances he plays the prophet and announces the depression: as Minister for the Colonies, he goes to Indo-China, a thing which had never before been done. Next he advises devaluating the franc—and he begins to tell the most unpleasant truths to his compatriots. He does not please, but he makes up for this with his surprises.

He also makes up for his short stature. For his native mountains, which he disowns, have turned him out a small man. To be small in the country is of little consequence, as long as one does as much work as a big booby; but to be small in Paris, when one is seen at the Law Courts, at the Chamber and then in the first rank of actors playing on the world stage, becomes a serious inconvenience. Small men who have been called upon to play a part in the world conceal the slightness of their stature by drawing themselves up and sticking out their chins as best they can; they force themselves into a manner of behaviour which influences their minds. Short men are fated to be presumptuous. In his party, the Democratic Alliance, Reynaud had a giant as leader, Pierre-Étienne Flandin, and naturally he detested him. Flandin, who is less heretical than Reynaud, naturally became Prime Minister before him, and Reynaud-David felled Flandin-Goliath. His very stature destines Reynaud boldly to take the offensive— and just as intensively as may be done in the Chamber.

For all his short figure, Reynaud received from his native mountains an iron constitution. The result is that overwork seems to have no effect on him. For a long time he used to bicycle in the Bois de Boulogne for half an hour, at seven-thirty in the morning, dressed in a sweater and knickers. In the alley which skirts Bagatelle, workmen pedalling at top

speed to get to their factories on time had no idea
that the cyclist whom they passed was the Minister
of Finances, and that he was over sixty. Having no
rugged slopes to climb on foot, as his grandfather
did, Reynaud worked his legs on a fine bicycle,
which he brought with him to his home on Place du
Palais-Bourbon after each half hour of exercise. And
once there, the cyclist turned at once into a bourgeois. . . .

A neutral journalist, after examining the biographical notices distributed by the Ministry of
Information, asked if it was true that Reynaud had
been three times around the world. When he received an affirmative reply he could not believe his
ears. He could not reconcile this vagabond turn of
mind with the picture one usually forms of a French
Prime Minister—the picture of a sedentary, whisk-
ered gentleman with a fat stomach.

Everyone in the Prime Minister's circle rejoices
that *she* is not to be seen; she is far from Paris at
present. But how long will she be away?

MARCH 23D

The Chamber greeted the new Cabinet icily. It
was known that the Radical party, in spite of Daladier's presence in the Cabinet, had a majority hostile to Reynaud. The Prime Minister thought it

would be clever to slip a flattering sentence about Daladier into his declaration; this did not thaw the opposition, but then the declaration lasted only four minutes, which is exceptionally short. This terseness was considered unseemly in the Senate particularly, as respect for form has not at all lost its empire there; the world crumbles to pieces and etiquette remains. . . . To tame the right wing, which had declared the Ministry to be "an indigestible and highly unseasonable cream tart," Reynaud spoke of the "treason of the Soviets," for he and Mandel have long been reproached with being "pro-Russian." On the other hand, an attempt was made to correct the impression of turbulence arising from a war government which contained thirty-five members, by announcing that a war committee had been formed; this comprised the Prime Minister and Vice Prime Minister, the Ministers of National Defence, of Finances, of the Colonies, of the Blockade and of Armaments.

Monsieur Frossard, Minister of Information (for at last, in the seventh month of the war, there is a Ministry of Information) brings it to our attention how curious it is that the Propaganda is not given a place in the committee. This is because it has not yet been understood that the Information is a war weapon, like the Blockade or the Finances.

Reynaud has grouped only 268 deputies; as 156 members of the Chamber have voted against him and 111 have abstained, there are 267 against the Government. That means the Cabinet obtained a majority of one vote. Reynaud deliberated for a long time as to whether he would resign at once, and then announced that he would remain in office. The Radical-Socialists, enemies of Reynaud, asked Daladier to resign, but he calmed the conspirators: the Ministry will fall as soon as the Chamber, which has adjourned for ten days, convenes again.

This beginning of the "Reynaud experiment," as people express it, is a great disappointment to the Prime Minister's friends as well as a source of uneasiness to those who wonder if we are about to have dozens of fragile ministries in war time, as we had in the worst days of peace.

The Prime Minister had a long interview with General Gamelin. Some great scheme, some startling feat, is looked for, because it would be an excellent thing to strike public opinion during the ten-day respite enjoyed while the Chamber is absent. But nothing has turned up. If the soldiers knew of the perplexity, I might even say the confusion, which actually reigns among the country's leaders, they would indeed be surprised. . . . They would also be astounded to learn that Reynaud chose the Ministry of Foreign Affairs . . . most reluctantly. He wanted to take over the Ministry of War, for that is the department which in his opinion, in war time, necessarily suits the Prime Minister best: one of Clemenceau's ideas. He would have called Colonel de Gaulle to his side and the younger school would have made its entry in the Rue Saint Dominique; and General Gamelin would have quit his post. But the thing was impossible, as Daladier's cooperation had been asked—just as it was impossible to send Gamelin away without provoking the instant departure of Daladier: these two men, however, Daladier and Gamelin, do not get on very well together even though they have joined together. . . . Gamelin, out of prudence, has up to this time shown himself very reserved, militarily speaking, and has not provoked the irreparable (an offensive, for instance) between the Nazis and ourselves. And Reynaud with his legendary "energy" frightens them; it is precisely that they fear he will bring about the irreparable. And that is why, at the Chamber and in the Ministry itself, the Prime Minister has such a large number of enemies.

However, the "irreparable" is not to be improvised with a snap of the fingers. All the talks that have taken place these past few days come to this: having a more "active" diplomacy, notably in Scandinavia and in the Balkans (in other words to speak more energetically to the neutrals who clandestinely give in to many of Germany's demands), speeding up the armament effort, making a few hostile remarks about the U.S.S.R. in public, increasing restrictions and more intensively organizing our war economy, etc. . . .

MARCH 26TH

Reynaud made a radio speech. He has not been able to announce very much, and he took up his

usual arguments on the necessity of "individual sac-
rifices." Comment by one of the ministry's sentries:
"He has an unsympathetic voice. I prefer Tino
Rossi."

MARCH 30TH

Reynaud has been to London and has placed his
signature at the bottom of a document by which
France and England bind themselves not to make a
separate peace. The first encounter with the British
Government was not a happy one; Chamberlain and
Reynaud do not "take to each other" readily.

Weygand's arrival in Paris leads to the conjecture
that Reynaud looks upon him as a successor to Gamelin. If this were to come about, no one knows what
would become of General Georges, Gamelin's second, who has been in difficulties all winter with the
Commander in Chief. Things have come to such a
pass that the General Staff has been cut in two, certain departments taken from Georges and assumed
by Gamelin; so that when an officer says that he belongs to General Headquarters, he is immediately
asked: "Which one?" The opposition of man to
man, department to department, which almost completely paralyzes the Administration, appears to be
developing also in the Army. On the other hand, the
offices of the War Ministry under Daladier seem to

have a fairly free hand and do not have the alarming moments familiar to other ministries. Under aspects of order, we have arrived at anarchy, for a condition where higher authority does not exist must be called anarchical. If Gamelin himself wants something, the offices can readily arrange to have the Generalissimo's wish remain a dead letter. And the offices risk nothing. In the same way, one cannot help noticing that at the Information, from rung to rung, no one fears those placed above them in authority; when the Minister has something to say, a good deal of "picking and choosing" takes place in the interpretation of his words; and the Minister himself, if the Prime Minister gives an order, can very well infringe it. To tell the truth, each one has come to take himself for a little tin god. . . .

Baudoin has been nominated Under Secretary of State to the Prime Ministry and Secretary of the War Cabinet.

R. gives me a bad piece of news: Hélène de Portes is back. And he shows me this sentence of Voltaire's on Madame de Montespan: [1] "This lady was not in on the secret; the King made a distinction between affairs of State and pleasures." And he added: "No, Reynaud is decidedly not Louis XIV."

[1] Favourite of Louis XIV.

APRIL 2D

———•◦•———

Publication of H. G. Wells' statement has been forbidden; indeed the statement was not encouraging . . . : "Decay is everywhere," says the author, "the morale of the people, which was very good during the 1914 War, is very mediocre today, etc. . . ." In the same manner, an earlier article by H. G. Wells was suppressed here; in this one Wells stated that in his opinion Mr. Chamberlain seemed incredibly conceited and incredibly ignorant. . . . At any rate, ignorance is not peculiar to the men of Whitehall, at least as far as Germany is concerned. (This ignorance, by the way, is part of the lack of interest among many English people for anything happening in foreign countries.) How many of our political men have the vaguest suspicion of what the Nazi movement really is? Even the greater part of those who denounced the Hitlerian danger have in mind a picture of a conquering Germany, very similar to the Germany of Wilhelm the Second. But things have been put on a very different footing by Hitler: conquest he wants, of course, but a universal revolution to his advantage must follow victory, if it does not precede it.

The Prime Minister has called a meeting of most of our diplomatic representatives in Central Europe, and the Ministry, in the course of this morning's conference, has decided upon certain measures for tightening the blockade. . . . In fact, an attempt is being made in several ways to show that "something is being done." But Reynaud himself has few illusions concerning the immediate efficacy of the blockade. A short while ago he found himself placed at lunch between the Minister of Blockade—at that time it was Pernot—and the Minister of Armaments, Dautry; Reynaud said with a smile that he counted more on his second neighbor than on his first to hasten the end of the war, and he developed this theory most brilliantly. . . . It seems that the blockade can be effective only in the long run.

Georges Bonnet is trying to rend the Ministry from within, that is, through Daladier's resignation, and he has succeeded in having the Radical-Socialist party send a delegation to the Minister of War to ask: "When are you going to trip Reynaud up? The sooner the better." It must be said that the opposition party has been encouraged in its bellicose designs by the news it has brought back from the provinces. During the few holidays which the deputies passed in their constituencies, they discovered once more that Reynaud was practically unknown to public opinion . . . or else that he was considered a schoolmaster with a nasal voice, always ready to punish the scholar, France. . . . Around Reynaud, this is all keenly felt and consternation reigns. (All the more as *she* has returned, runs in and out of the Quai d'Orsay as though she owned it and insists on giving her advice on all matters.)

The deputies have no idea in common, and allow themselves to be guided by negative considerations: "The cabinet (after ten days!) has not obtained the results which were to be hoped for, the mass of citizens don't care for it very much, so the Prime Minister must be defeated so as not to displease the electors, etc. . . . ."

Although Reynaud continues to bluff and show off, he feels at times that he is lost and that after a few days of power *he* is going to fall—as so many obscure prime ministers have done before him—*he* who dreamed of "changing all that" and of leading a "great ministry." The duration of a cabinet depends solely upon the value of the man at its head, he used to say. Can it be, then, that his character is far inferior to his intelligence? Or that our institutions, now that they are out of gear, condemn to impotence all new men, no matter who?

The first hypothesis is disturbing, particularly when one remembers that the two most "energetic" men of the regime, Mandel and Reynaud, were ministers at the time of Munich—that both of them protested, rightly or wrongly, against the policy then being followed—but they did not resign. They supported Bonnet's policy at that time, in spite of themselves, because of political "combinations," just as Bonnet followed the resistance party in September, 1939 and remained Minister of Foreign Affairs when war was declared. It would seem that by dint of being shaken up together in the curious cocktails which we call ministries, the political ideas of the different parties had lost their personal flavor. . . .

Our political men are interchangeable, and as those on the right wish to please the left and vice versa, it is hard to know where they stand. Attachment to principles has become purely nominal among most of them, and has been replaced by ingenuity in finding "piebald" formulas. . . . The English two-party system has the advantage of presenting very sharply defined boundaries; it also prevents such states of confusion as we are falling victim to these days.

And further, one deputy out of six is a lawyer; a very natural professional twist makes a lawyer see both aspects of a question only too readily, and he can plead for or against a subject with equal facility. This detachment might perhaps be tolerated in normal times; besides, it avoids the violence to which passionate convictions lead. But we are always obliged to return to this consideration: we live in a period of iron and fire . . . It is perfectly clear that our leaders are far from being the leaders that this critical moment calls for.

The metamorphosis does not take place: orators and critics do not change into men of action. And in all ages and in all spheres, war is the time for action. At the front and in the country back of the front, the same law of violence and swiftness is imposed upon all. *Vis et celeritas.*

APRIL 3D

———•◦•———

Reynaud did not change a word in his speech to the United States when I laid it before him for inspection; this surprises me, for as a rule he re-models with extreme minuteness the texts which are submitted to him. While he was talking to America in the large office of the Foreign Affairs Ministry, his daughter stood by his side; and he seemed to be talking just for her, which gave the scene an extremely congenial and charming character. "France," he said, "first of all represents a certain way of living. Everyone in our country can think freely and express an opinion without the least fear. And if opinions differ widely from one another, we see nothing regrettable in it; on the contrary we are proud of this marvellous French diversity, expressed in so many different ways in the architecture of our houses, in the costumes of our provinces, in the innumerable men of genius who have made French science, French literature, French art illustrious. . . . Let Germany keep that horrible *ersatz* of true religion which she calls the racial cult and the no less frightful *ersatz* of order which she calls Gestapo. Our art of living cannot put up with these substitutes. In France the priest or the minister is not thrown into prison because he serves another master than the state; in France a child is not torn from his family by the party in power and he is not forced, when the occasion arises, to denounce his parents. . . . No Gestapo in our country between citizen and citizen, between Aryan and non-Aryan, between man and God. . . ."

In the main, this is what France is fighting for, this is her only war aim: to live as before, in liberty, culture and well-being. And she is not made to understand this clearly enough.

APRIL 4TH

Example of a German propaganda stunt: a few weeks ago, Mr. Sumner Welles and Reynaud were photographed together at the Ministry of Finances; a map on an easel happened to be placed behind them. (Reynaud likes maps, even to the point of having one painted on a wall of his drawing room, Place du Palais-Bourbon.) In examining this photograph closely, one finds that the frontiers on the said map are placed any which way, that certain countries have even disappeared; in fact it is a medley of colors without any sense to it. For instance, Denmark forms part of Germany, etc. . . . The services of Dr. Goebbels have spread the legend that this is a map of post-war Europe already laid out, and that the diplomat had been invited to look at it. This

fable was published first by a Hungarian newspaper,
which allowed the Nazi press to take up the revela-
tion, which it, as a neutral daily, had printed. It
is so coarse and obvious that it seems too stupid to
be believed, but on the contrary, Hitler remarks in
Mein Kampf that it is *because* a thing is coarse and
obvious that it will be believed by many. Journalists
the world over constantly telephone us demanding
government explanations. The object of the photograph was sought for and examined, and it was
found to be an honest map of Europe scrupulously
possessing all of its pre-war frontiers; an investiga-
tion was made at the agency that photographed the
scene, and this is what was learned: because of their
coloring on the map, Russia and Germany formed
in the photograph a somber, impressive and united
mass. . . . Seeing this, the censor was alarmed and
asked that the colors be changed so as to make
Russia and Germany quite distinct from each other.
Then the photographer decided to cover the whole
of Europe with gouache colors, so as to have a
uniform shade everywhere; he thought thus to remove any ambiguous character from the document.
. . . But the frontiers disappeared during the operation, to his great despair, and he supplied them,
according to his fancy, in a series of most whimsical
dotted lines as though to prove the veracity of the
proverb that "A Frenchman does not know geogra-
phy." This insignificant occurrence was given front
page importance by the press all over the world for
twenty-four hours, on account of the racket made
over the incident by Germany. And as rectifications

were sent in too late, the effect on the majority of the public had been produced in the direction desired by the Nazis. . . .

It is confirmed that Gamelin, a few days ago, opposed the request made by Weygand for the creation of a front in the Near East.

APRIL 6TH

The plot unfolds, the stage is set: the Chamber leaves to the Senate the task of overthrowing the Cabinet. A debate will open on April 8th before the High Assembly, at the end of which Reynaud will be overthrown. It is believed that Daladier will return to power, although experience has proved that he did not direct the war with "growing energy." This means that the parliamentary machine has broken down completely; it is incapable of producing a government that can live, and can only reproduce one botched government after the other.

General Ironside has just granted his first interview. He declares that one may well tremble at the thought of what the Nazis could have achieved at the start of the war if they had undertaken an offensive in the West. But he assures us that we have turned the dangerous corner and if the enemy now launches an offensive on a grand scale we are ready to answer him.

A wind of panic sweeps over Holland and Scandinavia since the operations necessary to tighten the blockade have been decided. The neutrals bear a grudge against everyone; against Germany who terrorizes them and against England when the latter attempts to answer Germany.

At General Headquarters, "General Future" seems to have been put in charge; he is to have the bother of finding out how we are to defeat the Nazis militarily, and one often hears these days that "time is the fourth dimension of strategy."

APRIL 8TH

The Germans have landed in Norway and have occupied Denmark. For the latter operation it sufficed for her, as was announced, to "simply put in a telephone call." At a gala party given by the German Legation at Oslo on April 5th, a film was shown, marking the "exploits" of the German army in Poland, the "Baptism of Fire." The Norwegian Government did not give in but has been obliged to leave the capital. At seven o'clock in the morning Reynaud sent for Daladier and the Minister of the Navy, and promised the Minister of Norway the assistance of France. In Paris but one exclamation is heard: "The war has begun!" And most people add: "At last!" Anything seems preferable to waiting, to inaction, to the dun-colored war that has been experienced up to now.

APRIL 13TH

Hitler momentarily saves the French Cabinet. Seeing the invasion of Norway, the Senate rallied behind the Government after a declaration by the Prime Minister, in which he may be said to have fashioned for himself a springboard from these events. He took the responsibility of laying mine fields in Scandinavian waters and declared that Germany's road to Swedish iron ore was cut. A ghost rose from the Senate's benches, ninety-year-old Bienvenu-Martin who, in July, 1914, had had his hour of celebrity because he had been minister at the time, and in the absence of the Prime Minister had received the communications of the German Ambassador announcing war. This intervention was pathetic; it was as though the War of 1914 was exhorting the War of 1939. . . . On April 10th a long council was held, but the situation from a military point of view was not always made clear. On the 11th the success of the British Navy in Norway allowed Reynaud to read a sort of victory bulletin, and it took him barely seven minutes to conquer a recalcitrant public. He would have liked a vote and should have demanded it, but he missed out on a favorable occasion and allowed the Chamber to adjourn without going further. Weygand returns to Syria, and to mark the importance of the role which he may be brought to play, the telegram that the Prime Minister sent to the Commander in Chief of the Army of the Levant has been made public. Sending a message constitutes in itself an unusual procedure. Reynaud has moments of great uneasiness about the turn that military events are going to take, or rather, he does not see what the form of our intervention will be. His apprehensions are expressed in an interview which he agreed to give the New York *Times;* our censorship, raising its arms to heaven, allowed the publication of Reynaud's statements: "You would be more alarmed if we failed and if the Franco-British Fleet disappeared from the seas," said Reynaud. "Not for a single moment do I believe that this tragedy can happen. . . . However, let us all believe that war is on to the death. Nothing can stop it now, except defeat on one side or the other. . . ."

Before making his speech to the Senate, Reynaud was preparing it in his apartment on Place du Palais-Bourbon, and was trying to recall exactly the text of a celebrated sentence. The phrase was by Valéry: "We Civilizations now know that we are mortal." Reynaud began searching among the books in his library and turning leaves, in vain. Then Hélène de Portes rang up a number of people asking them for the reference. (I was not able to furnish it on such short notice.) These telephone calls made a very bad impression on me. How can a war leader spend his time polishing and repolishing a text, and studding it with quotations? It smacks too strongly of a Greek living in the days of Greece's end. And then (this makes me much more uneasy) Reynaud has adopted the custom of working far less at the Ministry and far more in his bachelor quarters, where it is difficult to reach him—and where *she* keeps good watch. . . . At the same time, politically speaking, he continues to walk a tightrope; he pays no attention, or very little, to the deputies' temper or frame of mind; he did not even know that his predecessors were in the habit of receiving eavesdropping police reports. He had to insist upon obtaining these reports, for they were not given him when he came to power; he is considered a transient person and as such is completely isolated. It should never be forgotten that bureaucracy, which remains in office, judges successive ministers with condescension and acts exactly as it pleases. All leaves have been suspended by the Command; this sign of coming great events surprises no one.

APRIL 22D

The Minister of the Navy, on being questioned about the British and French debarcations in Norway, made an elusive reply. It is not that he refuses to tell the truth, but that in spite of his position the truth is doled out to him most parsimoniously! The procedure is as follows: the Minister telephones to the French Admiralty and the latter replies that it has received no information from the British Admiralty. Thus the Ministry of Information can obtain no news about recent developments; and this time serious reasons excuse its silence.

We have been given a report which states that the German Fleet has lost 67 percent of its cruisers, 50 percent of its submarines and 33 percent of its pocket battleships; but the admirals say that these figures, though furnished by the Navy, are much exaggerated. . . . On the other hand, the Command is annoyed with Reynaud (and probably rightly) because the Prime Minister has declared that the first battle of the war has been won. That is to say, inflation of confidence is being practised. . . . But what government in war time is not forced into action of this sort?

The secret debates at the Senate on the 18th of April and at the Chamber on the following day have strengthened the Government's position. But Reynaud does not yet possess, properly speaking, any personal sway or influence over the house or the country. People are milling about him, not because of his personality but because the war is on in good earnest and that he represents France. At the Chamber, the Prime Minister made it understood, this time, that the Assembly should not adjourn, and a vote was obtained: 515 votes to 0. This is too splendid to be quite good; there should have been a little opposition and then the House would really have

done more towards making the Cabinet last by doing
. . . less. This is all most brilliantly explained by
specialists in parliamentary strategy, who certainly
have a lot of work on their hands. . . . It is said that
there are about sixty thousand Allied soldiers in
Norway.

APRIL 23D

The "green sheets" which bring us the text of the
German communiqués state positively that the lines
of communication of our expeditionary forces in
Norway are cut. This is alarming, for in this war
the Germans do not lie, *geographically*. When they
say that they are at such and such a place, the fact
is generally true, but they do exaggerate, for instance, in quoting the quantities of planes or materiel destroyed by their forces.

A newspaper recalls that in 1914 Germany was
already "interested" in Scandinavia. Wilhelm the
Second, as early as 1895, had told the future King
Gustavus the Fifth of Sweden that if any disorders
broke out, Germany would intervene, and that anyway the whole of the Germanic North was merely
one of Germany's flanks. Certain people, then, are
right: those who see in Hitler a Wilhelm the Second
who trims his mustache differently. . . . However,
Nazism is something different, something far more

serious, for it can take on a universal character, it is *contagious*. And one of our weaknesses lies in the fact that our democratic principles no longer have the communicative value which they had at the beginning; and beyond our frontiers they no longer have the effect they had after the French Revolution and during the whole nineteenth century. When the question of having revolutions *for* individuals arose, we were the first to lead the way, and spiritually the nineteenth century lived for a great part on the principles of our eighteenth century. On the other hand, during the twentieth century, at Moscow in 1917 and at Berlin in 1933, two great movements of ideas took the offensive, neither of which carried any further the tendency to emancipate the citizen but subjected him definitely to the State: this time, we were not the ones to launch the fashion.

Before the war, nothing showed more clearly the relationship between Communism and National Socialism than a visit to the museum of the Nazi Revolution, in Berlin. There one would find a whole series of documents on Bolshevism, and many curious objects arrested the visitor's attention, notably the uniform of the Communist party's storm troops in Germany, after 1918: it is the exact uniform of the Nazi storm troops, with the difference that the star takes the place of the swastika. . . . The truth is that the Nazis, in the political order, have done what thousands of German industrialists and manufacturers have so often done with such remarkable success: they have taken a foreign invention to exploit and develop. . . . With the success of the hammer and sickle, the Hitlerians have recognized the force of symbols and so have chosen the swastika (Hindu) and the eagles (Roman). They have realised the importance of mass manifestations, and the parades before Lenin's mausoleum have been highly perfected by the Nazis in the Nuremberg Congress and its illuminated cupola. . . . Führer equals Duce . . . Gay-Pay-Oo equals the model of the Gestapo. Hitlerian salute equals the Roman salute. Rosenberg equals Dimitroff. In the military order itself, the idea of parachutists was taken from the U.S.S.R., and the tank is an English and French invention, etc. (It is not imagination but *amplification* that Germans have in their blood.) And there was some truth in the joke that went around Berlin clandestinely before the war: "The Nazi is like a grilled steak, brown outside, red inside." Or again: "What is Marxism?"—"The non-Aryan grandmother of Nazism."

I have just learned that the Germans do not like the broadcasts I make from Paris for the B.B.C., and that one of their speakers called me a Pitt's agent.

APRIL 25TH

Reynaud is trying to prevent Italy from entering the war and Baudoin is helping him in this task.

The Prime Minister announced to the Commission of Foreign Affairs that "France must be ready to speak," but from what is said in Rome, Italy will refuse to enter into conversation. It is also said that the Comte de Paris would attempt to use his influence in Rome to delay the irreparable. It is not surprising that the Comte de Paris should try to second the efforts of the Government of the Republic, for this pretender, long before hostilities (in London in 1937), had told some Frenchmen who went to see him that in case of war the interests of France should be made to come before all questions of regime. . . . As the law forbids him to wear a French uniform or live in France, the Comte de Paris, it seems, has enlisted in the Foreign Legion under the name of Henri Picard.

That France, with all the power which she has at her command, should have allowed her relations with Italy to become what they are today, that is, the relation of victim to blackmailer, obviously brings judgment to bear on the French policy of recent years. If the sole continuous principle of French policy had not been horror of prestige, Italy would never have thrown herself into the German camp; today she would not be menacing us with passes and thrusts . . . with the German sword . . . if we had shown our sword sooner.

Indeed, in our diplomacy and more generally in the orientation of our general policy, our postulate seems to be: "Nations have entered the judicial age." So it is useless to re-read Machiavelli and learn his maxims: it would be like learning the rules of a drawing room game which is no longer played. So it is useless to make the State stronger: strong states are war machines and the times when these machines worked are over. . . . To tell the truth, those responsible had been well aware for several years that the mass of Frenchmen were feeding on dangerous illusions, but those responsible did not stop serving this dangerous food, because it suited their interests and their habits. . . . And when Munich, that number one blackmailing affair, awakened the French, a great many of these men were terrified by the simultaneous discovery of the danger and its extent, and thought that the best way not to attract the frightful menace brooding once more over their heads was to lie quiet. . . .

It was by ordering Italy to take some initiative that Germany broke the strongly fictitious atmosphere of truce which followed September 30, 1938. Rome suddenly claimed Nice, Savoy, Corsica, Tunisia and Djibouti. These demands were expressed in the course of a "spontaneous" manifestation which followed a speech made by Count Ciano in the Italian Parliament; the French Ambassador was seated in a box and remained there, instead of leaving the place at once. When one begins to practise an appeasement policy, as France and England did with Germany, it is impossible to know at first where this will lead, or how far. . . . We knew it at last on November 30, 1938: two months before that we had received a slap in the face from the Nazi gangster, who was stronger than we, and on that day we took a little cuffing from someone far weaker than we, the gangster's valet.

Since then, semi-official emissaries have been sent to Italy with a few presents to try to keep her in her state of non-belligerency. But Italy could not accept these presents, even if she had wanted to, for her German master forbade her to take tips. Our negotiators have not yet recovered from their failure. . . . The main idea of businessmen or bankers when they negotiate with dictatorships is this: the adversary always accepts a profitable compromise. The reasoning is that the adversary is the image of the person sent to come to terms with him, as though he also wore a top hat and frockcoat. This commercial postulate may be true in discussions in civilized periods, but it means nothing when the law of the jungle has become the law of international policy. What Bismarck foresaw in cases of this sort is proving true: "He who would buy off his enemies by concessions will never be rich enough."

MAY 2D

The British evacuate Andalsnes; the Franco-British expedition to Norway is apparently a complete fiasco. "It seems we don't know how to play the German game yet," says the military critic of the

Journal—but he was not allowed to print this in his article.

On learning of the defeat of the Franco-British expedition in Norway, Mandel said: "From catastrophe to catastrophe we will go on to final victory."

Criticisms of Chamberlain are becoming sharper and sharper. That there have been appeasers—be that as it may. But that they have been entrusted with the task of rearming the country and have become war leaders! . . .

Reynaud hopes that there will soon be a ministerial crisis in England; then he too could modify his list of collaborators, rejuvenate the *cadres*. (The other day, the old senator who is Minister of the Interior was suddenly sent for after dinner for an urgent council, but he refused the invitation. "After seven o'clock," he explained, "I must, according to my doctor's orders, put my slippers on and stay at home.")

In spite of present circumstances, the Prime Minister requires special justification for the great decisions he contemplates taking, and for this justification, as for most of those taken by his predecessors, he goes to London. Thus in recent years, before every serious difficulty, the French prime ministers have tried not to take any responsibility and have sought to leave the worry to the British Cabinet. The Downing Street telephone call was subterfuge number one (subterfuge number two was the journey to the League of Nations for a "council meeting"). The opinion that has long reigned in the Chamber is that a French minister could in no case adopt an attitude at odds with the British Ministry's, and France never got over her remorse at acting alone when the Ruhr was occupied, the only time she has ever proceeded independently. However, when she has asked advice in London, the French Government has generally plunged the British Cabinet into the most cruel perplexities, and the situation of the two allies mutually exhorting each other to plunge first would be comical, in other circumstances. For example, in 1936, after the reoccupation of the Rhineland, the French ministers went to the banks of the Thames and held long secret meetings with their colleagues and returned home, privately relieved, declaring that England would consent to nothing. But if France had acted first, English public opinion would have performed evolutions, I think. It has certainly let itself be influenced by the German *faits accomplis.*

The Franco-British Alliance, on which depends not only the liberty of France and England but the liberty of all Europe, has been constantly put out of tune by the "frightened little boy" attitude taken by French politicians. This attitude has increased the estrangement from France of certain important persons at Whitehall and in the City. And those who were pleased by this attitude, because it proved France's docility and lack of authority, calculated wrongly. They congratulated themselves that the "peril of French imperialism" was forever removed, as though France, a satisfied country after 1918, could be imperialistic! Curious as it may appear, they took the French for the Germans, as Lord

Tyrrell penetratingly observed one day, and the Germans for the English, for gentlemen with whom one could sign treaties.

MAY 4TH

Appeasement, at bottom, means one of the three following things:

1. I have understood nothing of the adversary's mentality.

2. I think that it is not worth while to die for one's country and I conceal this thought by saying that one must not be killed for the sake of others, for Czechs, for Danzig, for England, etc. . . .

3. Business first.

MAY 5TH

Saw Reynaud at Joan of Arc's festival, before the statue on the Rue de Rivoli. What a curious sight to see this dapper little man, with his cold "Oriental" mask, slanting eyes and sneering lips, doing homage to the national heroine. Here was scepticism saluting faith, politics bowing before mysticism.

Astonishing without end, in the case of Joan of Arc, is the extraordinary mixture of hope stronger than any reasoning and, at the same time, of rough peasant commonsense. The "important gentlemen" of the period proved to her, with excellent arguments in support, that the situation was hopeless, but this little shepherdess, who was inferior to them in birth and learning refused to be convinced by their sententious demonstrations. If one transfers the scene to our own day, it would mean suddenly bringing a peasant girl to the Prime Minister's house, having her meet General Gamelin and hearing her say to both of them: "No, you don't understand anything about it at all; the only thing to do is this."

But at the same time, this inspired young girl gives the most practical and precise indications and advice concerning the course to be followed. And, later, when the craftiest men of law submit her to the most perfidious examination, she baffles at every turn, with the most adroit and brilliant replies, those who wished to be rid of her. Has any virtuoso of parliamentary debates ever shown as much pertinency and such lightning rapidity of repartee as Joan of Arc during her trial?

Mysticism and reason; the two things were united in the girl who set France free. In those who have led France, at least in the best of them, for many years reason alone has spoken, and short-sighted reason at that. But of mysticism or, if one wishes, simply spiritual uplift—no apparent trace.

Politics have long since reduced the religion of
France to its most modest expression only: no more
high masses, but from time to time a low mass only,
for this cult. We have two national holidays or
feasts: Joan of Arc's and the Fourteenth of July—but
the first has never had the importance of the second.
The Fourteenth of July is the feast of "the pleasure
of leading an easy life in the most amiable country
in the world"; so long live the Fourteenth of July
with its illuminations, its bands and its booths! On
the other hand, Joan of Arc's feast is the celebration
of the most difficult virtues, the evocation of all the
efforts, of all the sacrifices which have made France
and which allowed her later to become the dancing
France of contemporary Fourteenth of Julys. The
mere idea of preaching in favor of effort and sacrifice is repulsive to the people's representatives, and
so they have given as little glitter and brilliancy as
possible to Joan of Arc's feast; this feast has all but
become a manifestation of the opposition in peace
time, and from an official point of view is an important ceremony in war time only.

MAY 6TH

When the Prime Minister's Chief of Staff was
leaving the Quai d'Orsay yesterday, he showed me
the deserted antechamber and lobbies and said: "The

Boss is there, but there is not even an usher to guard
him. . . . A few resolute, well-armed men could
kidnap the Premier with a snap of the fingers. . . ."
He added that he had tried to secure an adequate
guard but had been told that this would make a bad
impression. . . . The habits and setting of a good
little ministry of 1910 must be kept for the benefit
of the deputies who come here. . . . The other day,
one of Reynaud's collaborators, who had on the
captain's uniform that he had worn several weeks
before in the Maginot Line, accompanied the Prime
Minister to the Chamber. Some deputies afterwards
let this official know that the next time he went to
the Palais-Bourbon, he had better put on plain
clothes, so as to avoid giving offense to republican
susceptibility. . . .

MAY 7TH

Reynaud, in spite of the Chamber's absence, has
felt so strongly the unrest created by the recent news
of our defeats in Norway that he took the bull by
the horns and sought suddenly to call the House to
convene before the end of its holidays. The Prime
Minister's closer collaborators dissuaded him from
putting this idea into practice, for they believed that
the deputies would have overturned the Cabinet
without being impressed by the boldness of the

Prime Minister's initiative. In short, the position of the Reynaud Cabinet, which had improved with the invasion of Denmark and Norway, is secretly known to be most precarious. In the thick of the war we find ourselves in a state of embryonic ministerial crisis. The Government remains in office because circumstances prevent its being openly overthrown, but its life is worth little. It is like a criminal condemned to death who is granted a fresh reprieve from day to day. . . . Reynaud repeats his belief that things will improve for him, that the majority will crystallize, but he has moments of doubt and discouragement.

A few days ago, a most significant admission escaped him: "Ah! If I could buy peace once and for all, for a lump sum. . . ." All of a sudden the "strong man of France" was thinking like Daladier in his hours of greatest depression, talking like the partisans of a lame peace. It is certain that with the clarity of mind which is his, he sees that we are far from the goal, and that militarily the issue is not sharply defined. . . . On the other hand, several of his counsellors who do not believe in the possibility of victory murmur that "something must be arranged," without, however, giving the least indication of what compromise there could be. At the same time, the Prime Minister continues to preach of energy. This is not double dealing on his part, for at other moments he has strong hopes. It seems that *she,* for the time being, is bent on encouraging him, but it is possible that tomorrow she may change her tune. What does the Premier most good is to see a military leader who talks to him resolutely. Then he sees in himself an "animator" of victory. . . . However, he visits the Armies very seldom, and so is deprived of seeing the soldiers at close quarters and also of ascertaining on the spot if the generals have told him the truth. Perhaps he shows himself only seldom because he is not a man who communicates easily with the mass. He supposes that he is too reserved, too dry, and that his very assured manner prevents him from establishing real cordiality between himself and his hearers.

MAY 9TH

Yesterday some American journalists complained of the censor, also of many other things—and I must say that fair grievances and just motives for recrimination were not lacking. Sometimes it is their journey to the front which had been cancelled or put off. Sometimes a cable from the editor of their paper has been delayed or not delivered in good time. Or else they are persecuted by their concierges because they go out too often during the blackout. Each and every one of them moves me to pity before they question me, but this is playing the game fairly, although the technique of my interlocutors is never the same.

For instance, John Lloyd of the Associated Press, in gentle but sorrowful accents, confided his domestic troubles: Couldn't the Commissaire de Police in his quarter give him a little, just a little more gasoline? The Commissaire, called at once on the telephone, decided to consider this request favorably, for he solemnly declared: "Although Monsieur Lloyd is *only* a journalist, he shall have the gasoline ration due to doctors."

The New York *Times,* through the medium of Percy Philip, sends us conclusive reports pointing out what we should have done. Eric Sevareid, of the Columbia Broadcasting System, enlisted all sympathies. He had a couple of twins in Paris some weeks ago. And the other day, when one of us said that Paris might be bombed soon, we all had but one thought: "May the twins be able to leave Paris!"

Every man defends his own cause in his own manner, Knickerbocker with dynamism, Mowrer with passion, John Elliott with a smile, Edmund Taylor with irrefutable precision—not to speak of many others. Liebling of the *New Yorker* uses a weapon which is at once unexpected and peculiar: detachment. He comes into my office, talks about wines from Alsace, about the last *cassoulet* over which he licked his chops, about a novel by Malraux, and then he falls silent. From time to time, but always incidentally, he lets drop an allusion to the latest crimes committed by censorship. His air of apparent somnolence did not prevent his obtaining the most difficult and coveted favor of that time, a few weeks ago: a *tête-à-tête* with General Gamelin, a favor which has subsequently became very rare and very parsimoniously doled out. Before going to see the

Commander in Chief of the French Army, Liebling burrowed in textbooks of military strategy as though he were about to communicate a long report to Mr. Stimson instead of a "Profile" to the *New Yorker*. But the Tarpeian Rock lies close to the Capitol. Liebling's turn to be persecuted came when certain authorities discovered, when the war was eight months old, that he bore a German name; consequently it was decided that he could no longer go near the front. As he was undertaking a journey to an army then commanded by General Huntziger, we brought to the notice of the said authorities that General Huntziger also had a German name. . . .

As to Howard Clinton, another victim of our red tape, he is one of the most picturesque members of the journalistic profession. Arriving for the first time in his life in Paris, at the end of April, he did not know a word of our language: "This gives me a great advantage," he said to me at once, "since I can't *hear,* I *see* much better. My fellow journalists have all spent far too much time in France and they no longer feel that one thing which it is essential to communicate to their readers: surprise. Believe me, a well-gotten-up daily paper should change its foreign correspondents every six months. The ideal article—on Paris, for instance—would be written by a reader who had dropped from heaven to the banks of the Seine for the first time in his life. . . . My paper understands the situation rightly and has sent me over because I do not yet know either France or the French; this makes it possible for me to look at everything from a brand-new angle. . . ."

Years spent abroad as a foreign correspondent have made me familiar with the truth of Clinton's remarks. Not to know the language of the country in which one is residing certainly raises a good many inconveniences for a journalist; but on the other hand it offers many advantages, according to some people—avoiding errors of translation, in particular. I remember the case of one of my comrades on *Paris-Soir* who had been sent to Italy about five years ago, and had seen written up everywhere on the walls: "Viva Guerra!" From this remark he had drawn extremely pessimistic conclusions about Italy's war fever and had written a sensational article on the subject only to realize his error after the article was printed. "Guerra" was the name of a very popular bicycle champion at that time.

Errors of this kind were spared Clinton, for he announced his intention of making a great effort not to learn French—and he keeps his word to the end.

He had not brought a dictionary with him, but as a sort of compensation, before leaving New York, had scribbled a few odds and ends of sentences on a leaf of a notebook. When he arrived, he showed me this scrap of paper, on which were the following mysterious annotations:

> *Mère Filloux*
> *Picasso*
> *French cancan girls*

And a little further down on the page, in French:

> *Cherchez la Femme*

He saw my disconcerted expression and explained that "Cherchez la Femme" was a recommendation made to him before he left New York: it was useless to enter too much into detail concerning French interior politics, he had been told, it was sufficient to know the names of whatever "girl friends" had an influence over the ministers. As to the first three headings, these stood for articles of potential interest to the public, for even the war itself no longer furnished enough copy and was just a "phoney war." Alas, Clinton spoke thus to me in April, and a few days later the war started in earnest in Norway.

MAY 10TH

Ça y est! one hears little else in Paris since this morning. In other words, Germany invaded Holland and Belgium at dawn. A great many towns and aviation hangars have been bombed in France itself: Nancy, Calais, Lille, Abbeville and Lyons especially; and there has been much artillery fire from the enemy along the front. The Cabinet has met but the meeting of the Ministerial Council has been postponed. The man in the street feels much more confident than the leaders, be they political or military. The Army has gone to the help of the Belgians in an operation foreseen in January. A surprising decision on the part of Gamelin, considering his prudence, and also the remark which he so often made all winter: "The first one of us, Germans or French, who leaves his shell is lost." Perhaps the Commander in Chief has abandoned his doctrine because he felt that the pressure on the Prime Minister as well as on the simple private, in favor of an intervention, was too strong to resist. It is said that he is no man to remain alone in his opinion, and when the expedition to Norway was decided upon, he declared: "I yield to the pressure of public opinion and I wash my hands of the whole matter."

A very exciting moment came when the entry of French and English troops into Belgium was known. Our sole reason for hope lies in the Army, in which for years we have had immense confidence and in which we continue to believe. There is one cloud in the sky: the weakness of our aviation, of which we are all aware. Many rumors are afloat; it is said that the Germans have reached such and such a place, but no reliable news has arrived to confirm this. All we know is that after they had dropped parachutists over several Dutch aviation fields, they secured possession of the terrain with great ease; big transport planes arrived by tens and landed German troops in the suburbs of The Hague. The Dutch and Belgian governments have refused the Nazi ultimatum demanding their resignation, and Grand Duchess Charlotte has left Luxemburg.

Reynaud has seized the opportunity of making his peace with the right wing of the Chamber and has asked Louis Marin and Ybarnégaray to become State ministers; this they could not refuse to do. London is in the midst of a cabinet crisis: Chamberlain is resigning and it is foreseen that Churchill will at last come into power. Gamelin's position has been "consolidated" by Hitler (just as Reynaud's was on April 9th) and he has sent his troops an Order of the Day, in which he recalls that he had foreseen the present offensive from the beginning of the war. General Headquarters, the office of operations, is much preoccupied by the fact that collaboration with the Belgian and Dutch armies must be almost completely improvised.

Hitler declares in a proclamation that the events about to take place on the battlefield will decide the fate of the German people for a thousand years. This is his figure; he has often quoted it before. This is the space of time which he expects his regime to endure, no more, no less. In the evening, Reynaud spoke over the air: "The French Army has unsheathed its sword, France communes with herself, etc. . . ." It is estimated that thirty German divisions are on the march in the Low Countries.

MAY 12TH

One of the forts of Liége, Eben Emael, has been taken by the enemy, who is reported to have succeeded already in crossing the Meuse on one side and the Albert Canal on the other. This means ruin to the hopes of the Command, which had counted upon a much longer resistance. The German tanks cross either over bridges which were not destroyed (having been taken by surprise) or over pontoons. . . . At Amsterdam and Rotterdam, groups of Fifth Columnists have been seen emerging from certain buildings, firing on the police and preparing the way for parachutists.

Went with an American columnist to see Dautry in his office. The Minister of Armaments is not depressed, although some of the factories have been somewhat damaged already, but telegrams received from production heads are very encouraging: "Production will continue at normal output in spite of damages. . . . Morale of workmen excellent, etc. . . ." When the conversation turns on machines and planes ordered in the United States, the Minister's face grows somber, for a good deal of time must elapse before important quantities of these can be delivered. An enormous mistake has been made, the mistake of planning as though we could be sure of holding out for years; and also, it was decided for economy's sake to build factories in France and to buy machine tools in America. Hence, long delays. . . . It had not been considered that this would take not only time, but soldiers who would have to be recalled from the front and sent to factories. When I asked Dautry what he needed most from America, he answered: "Everything." No comments are necessary.

All the under-secretaries of State have been suppressed. The Government is decidedly a "continuous creation"; new ministers are added unceasingly

to the original list. This impresses the public most
unfavorably. It would be far better once and for all
to have a restricted War Government, a sort of
Committee of Public Safety, but Reynaud, with his
prudence, will not come to this decision except by
slow degrees.

When the Ministry of Information had to announce to journalists the bombing of various parts
of the country by German aviation, it received orders from the Command to intimate that the enemy
had aimed at military objectives alone. The truth is,
even if such had been the intention of the bombing
planes, no raid has ever been made which bore ex-
clusively upon military objectives, for many bombs
miss the designated targets or fall short of them,
wrecking houses, killing civilians . . . so this is a
question of interpretation, frankly. It is confirmed
that Nancy has suffered severely during the last two
days from bombings.

MAY 14TH

Bad news. At the military conference at the Ministry of War, before the foreign journalists, the attempt has been made to attenuate as much as possible a truth which surpasses our worst fears. The
great blow had to do with the Corap Army. Once
more the Sedan region is synonymous with disaster.

The reserve troops who were there rejoined their positions late and did not hold very firmly the positions in which they were previously settled. This German advance, undertaken at a point that was not expected—because it was believed that the Ardennes would slow up the motorized columns so considerably that they would take another way—imperils the army commanded by General Giraud, which has already entered southern Holland. The refugees who throng the Belgian roads greatly impede the British troop movements. French tanks have encountered German tanks in Belgium near Saint-Trond, but ours were too few. In all, about fifteen hundred machines confronted one another. We lack tanks everywhere, and try to use as few as possible of those we have, so as to reserve them for the decisive moment. . . . I recall a remark of Daladier's about Gamelin before the war; it was repeated to me then but I paid little attention to it, far too little: "What can I do about it? Gamelin doesn't *like* tanks."

As to planes, an officer returning this evening from the battle says that the remark most often made by our soldiers is, "But where are our planes?" And eyes are lifted to the sky where only German planes appear, flying low to machine gun columns of fleeing civilians and columns of soldiers alike.

It is in the middle of a battle, and a battle unevenly fought, that the question of the coordination of orders between the French, British and Belgian armies must be solved as well as possible. In principle, the British Expeditionary Force has long been under the orders of the French Commander in Chief, but the British aviation remains free to lend or withhold assistance at such and such an operation, when this help is asked of it. Daladier has been to see King Leopold to try and regulate the aspect of the problem which concerns the Belgians; for it is impossible to fight against a single German army with several armies obeying separate orders. Today we are paying terribly dear for the weaknesses which allowed Belgium to leave the Anglo-French orbit and endeavor to take an independent position. This independent position, from a practical point of view, is greatly to Germany's advantage. Later on it will no doubt be difficult to explain how the democracies, after the terrible lesson of 1914, could have left Belgium out of their military control. Lack of the instinct of preservation in democracies will surely bewilder future generations.

What has apparently happened in several Dutch towns is sickening; with coldblooded brutality the Germans have killed and destroyed furiously. The numbers of civilian victims that are quoted are so considerable that one dares not believe them to be correct. . . . Thousands of the Dutch have crossed Belgium and, together with far more numerous Belgians, are fleeing over the roads into France.

MAY 15TH

Since the taking of Sedan, the battle of the Meuse is called the "Battle of Frontiers." . . . The German bridgeheads have been attacked, but unsuccessfully, and tanks continue to come up as reinforcements to the river banks now solidly held by the enemy. . . . The Commander of the Dutch Army, Winkelman, has asked for a cessation of hostilities, but it is understood that Queen Wilhelmina's Fleet will continue to defend the Dutch Colonies.

It is believed that the Germans have at least ten thousand tanks: we are supposed to have sixteen hundred only. As to the proportion of planes, it stands at about one French plane to nine German ones.

A rumor was spread in Paris that the retreat at Sedan was intentional, that a counteroffensive would be launched at any moment to menace the enemy's flanks; but a checkup of all information ascertained that there was no question of an undertaking on such a scale. However, people cannot be prevented from keeping the mirage of the Marne in their eyes: even the most sceptical people dream of a repetition of the miracle, as though miracles could be reproduced at will.

General Giraud is now in command of the Ninth

Army, General Corap having been put on the shelf. The retreat of the army which advanced into Belgium seems to proceed under great difficulties. Curious to relate, it was learned that during its advance this army was never bombed by the Germans. . . . And still no agreement with the King of the Belgians by which his army would be subordinated to the French Command: the principle of "every man for himself," which was that of pre-war diplomacy, now extends into military matters.

MAY 16TH

The Sedan pocket, which was thought to have been filled in, was reduced by our forces for only a very short time and has quickly taken on considerable proportions: it is now sixty kilometers wide and twenty kilometers deep. A word begins to circulate, at General Headquarters and at the Ministry of War, the word "Infiltration." This is a euphemism to indicate the columns which in a fan-shaped movement enter the interior of the French lines, disorganizing the army's rear, cutting our communications, etc. . . . and opening the way for the bulk of the German infantry. A colonel from General Headquarters went to see the Minister of Information and told him, "This is like what happened in Poland."

In the ill-lighted corridors of the Ministry, lugubrious meetings and parleys are held. It was learned this morning that the Ministry of Foreign Affairs had received an order to burn its archives and, at the end of the afternoon, I noticed that the lawn back of the Ministry was covered with ashes. I went to the Quai d'Orsay at a quarter past seven this evening to ask a trifling service of an usher, but he replied: "I finish my work at seven." Life continues pretty much as usual for most people here, for they do not realize the extent of what is happening. The earth is quaking close by, and most average Frenchmen wish to go on winding up their clocks and dusting their furniture. And so those in Paris who *know* have the impression that they are living in a nightmare, particularly today, now that precise information about the proportions of the catastrophe has reached the capital. When one of us announced that the Germans were at Laon, he was cold-shouldered and dubbed "defeatist," but alas, it is true that the Germans are at Laon.

Another word frequently used by military experts is *colmater*.[1] However, General Headquarters keeps extremely calm, and this "warping" process is spoken of as though it were child's play. Reynaud, whose patience is exhausted, wishes to displace General Gamelin, but he only hinted at the matter this afternoon at the Chamber, so as to note its reaction to the decision. He spoke of "changing men and methods," of taking "revolutionary measures"—but, once more, the speech preceded the act. In reality, his

[1] Which means to stop up a gap.

energy is only a façade, and since March 21st, that
is, for fifty-six days, he has done nothing but flounder
in the parliamentary quagmire, just as a Prime Minister would have done in . . . 1912. He has not been
able to make a single important decision, and he
hangs on as best he can. It is true that the Terrible
Hour says to him: "I am too great for you."

This evening he spoke over the air and denied
that the Government was thinking of leaving Paris
—and even in spite of the fact that he had learnt
from the Commander in Chief this afternoon that
the Germans had marched on Laon and *that nothing could stop their progress if they chose to advance immediately in the direction of the capital.*
General Gamelin stated before the Prime Minister,
the President of the Chamber and the President of
the Senate that he could no longer answer for the
security of the Government, and advised its evacuation.

British aviation bombs the Ruhr when it would be
far more urgent to bomb the German columns marching over French soil. . . . Parisian restaurants are
brightly lighted inside and as animated as usual, and
tonight the Champs-Elysées was alive with cars. . . .

In their communiqué the Germans announce that
they have widened the already broad salient which
they have opened in the French lines and that they
are continuing to enlarge it. They announced the
capture of Reims, but it seems that the town has
only been evacuated, which permits Reynaud to declare that the Germans are not in the city. Reynaud's
two statements have been, on the whole, very pru-

dent—and it is this very prudence, or, more exactly, this smallness in everything, that has inspired political or military leaders to put France in her present situation. Smallness on the part of the Commander in Chief who has not been able to exact what he needed from the British, as Foch did in 1918; smallness in the General Staff in its general plans; smallness in the head of the Government who does not even give a warning cry of alarm, and contents himself with presenting the situation under none too somber colors. If the path of prudence at any price is chosen, then one must remain logical with oneself to the end and not commit the "imprudence" of entering into a war. . . . Truly, the "change in men and methods" and the "revolutionary measures" should have taken place several years ago. . . . Thousands of my compatriots believed, four or five years back, that the preservation of our institutions, no matter what their defects, was preferable to a change; and today they realize that we were far more dangerously ill than was believed, and that only a most energetic cure could have saved the Republic. Heard an astounding conversation on the subject tonight between left wing Frenchmen. A new factor: rising anger.

MAY 17TH

A report has been communicated to us explaining
how the Germans were able to build pontoons and
get their tanks across. First of all, thanks to their
aviation, they silence the French artillery batteries
which hold the heights above the river. So it is the
mastery of the air in full daylight which has assured
the success of their attempts. . . . Our aviation,
whose delays were considerably aggravated by the
Popular Front administration, has never since then
made up for lost time, and today can do scarcely
anything, in spite of the extraordinary courage shown
by the pilots. When one reflects that the Minister
of Aviation under the Popular Front, Pierre Cot,
was a Radical-Socialist, and that the Minister of
War, Daladier, belonged to the same party, the responsibility of this party of mediocre men and ideas
looms enormous in the face of actual reverses. It is a
party of good, short-sighted people, cramping everything they touch, giving at once a debonair, unkempt
and petty-bourgeois idea of France and her empire.
"But France is Radical-Socialist, Monsieur le Maréchal," we had said to Lyautey. "Yes, and that might
be her death," was the reply. May this prediction
never come true!

The German "pocket" is much more than that:

it is now over one hundred kilometers wide. On the other hand, Brussels, Mechlin and Namur have fallen into the hands of the enemy. . . . And still no counter-offensive, in spite of so many rumors to that effect. Today, at the hairdresser's, a customer with a good honest face sharply scolded an attendant who was trimming his beard for saying that events were taking a bad turn: "We are laying a trap for them . . . you'll see . . . it will be like 1914. . . ." And he quoted the Order of the Day sent out by Gamelin this morning, "Win or die, etc. . . ." It was the average Radical-Socialist in this customer who protested, who wished to see things just as lovely as they had always been shown him up to the present. . . .

Censored an article by a neutral which stressed an awkward sentence from the speech pronounced yesterday by Reynaud: "We must immediately forge new weapons." It is high time, when one is seriously wounded, said the journalist with reason, to call for weapons: were there not sufficient weapons to begin the struggle? . . . Speaking of weapons, rumor had it, when the battle began (it is now called the "Battle of France") that our tanks were of better manufacture than the German tanks and resisted attacks better than theirs. But it seems, unfortunately, that this is not true. And further, we lack anti-tank weapons. This winter's effort in armament manufacture seems to have been directed towards heavy artillery. *Preference has not been given to the output of the arms which won the war in Poland,* as the younger clan in the General Staff had demanded. The old school, today overwhelmed by this terrible invasion of motorized and mechanized troops, the possibility of which it had denied, talks in disdainful tones of the "fluidity" of conditions. Disdainful because, first of all, this "fluidity" was denied in the books. . . . Indignation against the Commander in Chief and against Daladier increases hour by hour in the Chamber, and the deputies are now ready to sacrifice those whom they have maintained for years in the highest offices.

MAY 18TH

Berlin announces that the German Army is now ninety miles from Paris, and our command says, "No, a hundred kilometers from Paris"; however, it would seem that the invaders are not heading for the capital: they prefer to form a wedge between the British Expeditionary Force and our armies. My brother left yesterday for the North by a road which goes through Amiens, and I wonder whether he will have been able to reach Arras. The German propaganda underlines the fact that in 1914 it took the Imperial Army sixty-six days to take Antwerp, and that this time nine days were sufficient for the Nazi Army. However, Belgian garrisons in the forts still are resisting, and King Leopold has sent them a message exhorting them to hold out.

Reynaud has obliged Daladier to leave the Ministry of War—but asked him to take the portfolio of Foreign Affairs. With this last decision he sinks even lower in the esteem of those who have had confidence in him. The Germans had to be at Laon, already, before the Prime Minister had the "courage" to eliminate Daladier from the post in which he proved to be the blow to the regime—and the conclusion of this long and unfortunate experience is that Daladier is about to direct the foreign policy of France.

The case of Paul Reynaud shows that intelligence, unless accompanied by character, is counterfeit coin.

The French democracy has become a regime with neither obligations nor sanctions. No matter who can be placed no matter where, and do no matter what at no matter which moment. . . . Reynaud has taken on the Ministry of War, but he has so little personal influence when so much is needed that he has asked Marshal Pétain to become Vice President of the Minister's Council; the latter has accepted. Mandel is given the Ministry of the Interior, General Giraud is placed in command of a group of armies—the "strong and enterprising men" are coming into office—at the eleventh hour, or at any rate at a time when the situation (such as the Prime Minister himself described it to be today over the radio) is "serious, *but* not hopeless." The immediate "departure" of General Gamelin is expected.

MAY 19TH

Reynaud has asked Weygand to succeed Gamelin. In what condition will he find the French Army? It is thought that the Germans, who are at Saint-Quentin, have in one week thrown eighty-five divisions into the battle, twelve of which are motorized.

Everything seems to be lost, so the voters are no longer treated so cautiously as before: twelve hours of work a day have been decreed in the aviation factories. What a revenge *things* have taken over *men!* Indeed, everything must mathematically be paid for in politics, and the ordered sloth of 1936 ends in *in extremis* overwork in May, 1940.

The Secretary General of Foreign Affairs, Alexis Leger, has learned, it seems from the newspapers, that he has been displaced. This change had been under way for some time and was decided at one of the restricted little councils held by Reynaud in his Place du Palais-Bourbon flat, councils at which *she* assists and where she gives her opinion in no uncertain voice. The President of the Republic created no difficulties and signed all the new decrees of the last few days, but he looked very shocked when it was decided to remove General Gamelin. . . . Naturally, the most diverse rumors have been rife since the departure of the Commander in Chief (suicide, arrest, etc. . . .) and the mass, as the extent of our reverses is revealed, obeys the usual reflex and cries: "It is the fault of traitors!" Indeed, it is impossible to believe that the French Army could have been placed in such a position unless paralyzed by leaders sold to Germany. Ignorance and stupor remain the most widespread emotions here, while anger grows hotter among more and more numerous groups.

MAY 21ST

Two officers who bring eye-witness narratives from the battlefields have come to the usual conclusion that the Germans can do what they want, on account of their complete air superiority. First of all they take photographs to find out the exact positions of dispersed French troop elements, after which they send up their Stukas; these pounce down upon the said elements, who cannot reply; it is only then that the motorized units preceding the bulk of the army appear. . . . Conferences in which the situation must be explained to American journalists, so as to lessen its gravity in their eyes, have become a real trial, and I come out of it very badly. . . . Amiens is taken, so is Arras, and I have no idea where my brother can be.

General Giraud has been made prisoner in the course of one of his visits to the field of battle. Thus, the French chief whose name had become a synonym for mobility and offensive has been taken from France at the very moment she most needed him, and Reynaud is much affected by what has happened to the boyhood friend in whom he placed so much hope. It had so often been said of Giraud: "He will be the Foch of this war." And some people thought that, if the occasion arose, he could have played a political role.

During the winter Giraud had commanded a reserve army, and it was only when things turned out badly in the North that he was given a prominent position. He was, with Huntziger, among those on whom one counted in difficult moments.

The Army of the North and the British are now cut off from the bulk of the French Army; a disaster seems no longer avoidable. The General Staff says that we must hold the Somme River. But will we have the time to establish ourselves in strong positions? In his speech to the Senate Reynaud attempted to explain matters at length and to persuade his hearers that all was not lost. His voice was assured, his bearing as firm as usual (political men evidently have a capacity for "taking" any kind of situation without appearing moved). "Incredible mistakes have been committed and these will be punished," he cried. But this verbal energy makes very little impression on anyone, now. Already the Prime Minister had announced that in future the penalty for certain defaults or neglect would be death—but so far he has contented himself with loud shouting. If really "incredible" faults have been committed, then why not announce them, together with the execution of the culprits? Reynaud is incapable of showing the fierce energy required for a situation such as this; he wishes to act, but lets obstacles stop him, and contents himself with announcing that he is going to act. . . . In this speech of Reynaud's can be found the severest judgment ever passed in recent years on the doctrines of the "old school" General Staff: "To our classical conception of war," said Reynaud, "a new conception is opposed, that which calls principally for planes and motorized units." It could not be stressed more clearly that most of the official thinkers of the "Ecole de Guerre" have been taken by surprise and have lacked imagination.

The same *status quo* has reigned alike over the brains in military command and political brains. . . . How can this partial halt of French intellect be explained, when this same intellect continues to make great progress in all domains that do not concern the Commonwealth—in literature, science, art, etc.?

The principal reason for this halt undoubtedly lies in the fact that superior authority is feared no longer, and has faded away. Thus there has been no stimulus. A functionary who knows that nothing can make him lose his job, does the minimum amount of work and tries to avoid the nuisances that strew the path of the zealous. Advancement was by seniority, scarcely ever through choice, so what reason was there to distinguish oneself? Careers were mathematically laid out, the routine of daily work was comfortable and a pension was assured; there was nothing to do but to glide along on greased wheels, in accordance with habits contracted many years before. . . . No innovations, in anything! This bureaucratic state of mind governed the entire Administration, and it was not for transient, vacillating ministers to change anything there. It was not known, however, that this bureaucratic spirit had reached the Army too; the defeats of the last ten days have revealed all this to us.

After Reynaud's speech the old senators went off dismayed, some of them hanging their heads like culprits. For Reynaud had uttered heartrending sentences: "France cannot die. . . . If you tell me that tomorrow a miracle alone can save France, then I will reply that I believe in miracles because I believe in France." This last declaration, so unexpected from the lips of a rationalist such as Reynaud, seemed to him to fit the present circumstances, but it was a thought invented by his ingenious mind, not a cry emerging from the depths of his soul.

MAY 22D

Today, a ray of hope: Arras has been recaptured. And General Weygand's visit by plane to the Army of the North, a visit which exposed him to great danger, creates the impression that a real chief has taken command. Alas, everyone has turned into an amateur strategist, and it is whispered that the Germans have most incautiously exposed their troops, that a counterattack could change the aspect of things. . . .

The serenity of Paris—where the spring is more beautiful than ever before—is astounding. Evidently the Parisians do not realize how matters stand, but there are many persons among them who do understand, and yet keep to their confidence in the future of the country, certain that the sun will rise again tomorrow and that France will be there also.

The flight of peasants all along the roads was provoked by German agents disguised as beggars, blind men, French wounded, etc. . . . who came on ahead of the enemy, terrifying the populace with their tales. All this to block the roads with armies of civilians and to render highways impassable to French reinforcements.

A far-fetched, subtle sentence of Reynaud's: "If we can hold out a month, we will hold out long enough, and we will have travelled over three-quarters of the road which leads to victory." What does he mean? Churchill has been to Paris and saw Reynaud and Weygand this morning at the Ministry of War. The interview was dramatic. The British Expeditionary Force, being surrounded, wishes to be evacuated as quickly as possible from the north of France and return to England. The liaison between the action of British aviation and the action of the Anglo-Franco-Belgian Army in the North remains extremely imperfect.

A curious scene is frequently enacted in the lob-

bies of *Paris Mondial,* the State short-wave station
whose broadcasts are aimed particularly at the
United States. An American comes in with a text
to be broadcast in which he calls for planes and arms
for France. The censor, throwing up his hands to
heaven and invoking American neutrality, pitilessly
deletes these appeals. This quite naturally makes the
author of the appeal furious. . . . The censor then
justifies himself as follows: "Only think," he tells
me, "only imagine what would happen if I allowed
such harangues to go through and if *one* listener
heard them. We would be plunged into the greatest
difficulties." Of course the good man exaggerates
in counting upon only *one* listener but it unfortunately remains true that *Paris Mondial* raises a very
timid voice indeed, whereas DJL, DJD, DXB, the
German stations, reach a numerous public, thanks
to powerful technical apparatus.

MAY 25TH

Weygand has displaced fifteen generals. The expected counteroffensive which was to be launched
by General Gort and General Blanchard has not
taken place and the impression persists that the
Franco-British war machine is paralyzed. It really
leads one to believe that popular instinct is not at
fault, and that sabotage on a grand scale has been

done. . . . In any case, it is certain that great executive difficulties have been encountered, such as in-
here in all coalitions. It was the same in the last war,
but it was said that arrangements had been made to
prevent the recurrence of such difficulties; however,
it appears that this machinery is not yet perfect. . . .
Was it not repeated, in Paris and in London, that
"there was plenty of time," and was it not secretly
believed that there would be no war? And so, under
these circumstances, why prepare for something
which was not going to happen? . . .

If some genie, through the years preceding the conflict, could have lifted the roofs of houses and seen
what was happening in chancelleries and general
staffs in Paris and Berlin, he would have noticed
that across the Rhine a great plan was being fever-
ishly worked out—the conquest of Europe—and that
in the democratic countries there was no unity of
design. . . . It was thought after the war that the
French and British teams could work together thoroughly and in full accord, but nothing of the sort
has happened.

The Belgians are in a very bad situation. However, it would seem that our troops have succeeded
in drawing nearer to the encircled army, but without reaching it. Weygand has gone to Dunkerque
by plane, wishing to find out for himself how things
stand. The aviator who took him there felt very
uneasy, on account of the heavy responsibility. The
General wore a little khaki cover over his oak-leaf
embroidered képi, and in spite of his age—he is
seventy-three—he seems to stand rather well the gi-

gantic efforts required of him under present circumstances.

Meanwhile, Mandel is displacing prefects and arresting supposed Fifth Column accomplices, and has decided that everyone shall work fifty-two hours a week in all the ministries. Another boomerang from 1936. . . . The forty-hour week gives way before the fifty-two-hour week, and the offices are obliged to keep open twelve hours a day. Why weren't these measures taken at the beginning of the war? The Prime Minister would have made himself unpopular if he had done so, and he refrained. And when Daladier left power, a deputy (Isoré) made this unforgettable remark: "Perhaps his successor will not direct the war so democratically. . . ." Democracy had completely lost its significance, for this deputy, and was now no more than a synonym for "negligence" and "sloth."

MAY 26TH

A strange procession today in the streets: the shrine of St. Genevieve was paraded through Paris, in accordance with a very ancient tradition which demands that the patroness of the capital be displayed to Parisians when the invader is at the gates of the city. In the crowd all classes are mingled, reconciled. . . . And only a month ago distinctions still subsisted. Up to the very eve of the German offensive, remarks like this could be heard in the workmen's quarters: "The war is just an excuse to rob working men of the advantages they have gained over past years. . . ." Today, those who belonged to the political right or left, those who had possessions and those who had nothing at all, all feel menaced equally, and were represented in the crowd which knelt before the Saint's shrine as it was carried through; the same crowd listened to the voice of the clergy, and repeated litanies and prayers, and sang hymns. . . . The event makes one realize that every Frenchman is a pawn in the terrible game now being played: every Frenchman, with all that he possesses: beliefs, houses, ideals, pensions, social insurance, etc. . . .

The very truth is that only events as they happen can teach what has been predicted without success by numerous prophets. No one has noticed the lesson in humility given to the press by the blindness of the French during recent years. True, a great part of the press did not sound the alarm too loud, lest it displease its readers too much, and the cowardice of some newspaper editors equalled the cowardice of the politicians who would not touch off a warning bell. Nevertheless, it remains that numerous dailies untiringly denounced the German peril without succeeding in rousing the nation. Why? A Frenchman is neither stupider nor less patriotic than other men. Then what?

Perhaps because the printed word has lost a great deal of its power. By dint of multiplying great, sensational headlines, of announcing scoop upon scoop, the press has led the public to become profoundly sceptical. The press, which in the nineteenth century could foment revolutions in France, no longer provokes anything more than smiles—or yawns of boredom. The horror of being a dupe, a feeling that used to belong only to the intellectual classes of France, is now shared by deep layers of the population. And since, on the other hand, the faculty of indignation, as well as idealistic impulses in general, have become far rarer than before in our democracy —and in all modern democracies—the result is a profound detachment on the part of the citizen toward all public events. The average Frenchman considered himself primarily a spectator. That is why today's ceremony, where all who assisted would have liked to take part and sacrifice themselves for the good of the country, was so curious. As St. Genevieve's shrine passed by, those who had thought themselves "detached" felt attached once more to the entire French community and in union with the merest stones of the threatened city.

MAY 27TH

Reynaud has been to London to see Churchill and has mentioned the possibility of an armistice. The evacuation of the Army of the North will be

made at Dunkerque. This is going to be a considerable enterprise, with German planes bombing the
transports without respite. It is feared that one hundred thousand men will be left behind as prisoners.
. . . On account of the confusion organized by the
Germans (telephone calls ordering evacuations and
purporting to come from the prefects, whereas really
originated by German agents, etc. . . .), the disorder
which reigns up there is frightful. Still no news of
my brother. Calais is on the verge of giving in to
enemy pressure and the resistance apparently put up
by a small group of English soldiers there is remarkable.

There have been two Cabinet meetings, the second one provoked by the King of the Belgians' decision to ask for an armistice. A little earlier, Belgian
Prime Minister Pierlot, who had come to Paris,
spoke on the radio and it was widely noticed that
in his speech, while he manifested his government's
intention of fighting to the finish, he made no mention of the King. When he had quitted the King,
the latter still clung to the same attitude: to remain
with the army and give up a useless struggle. The
King's political perspicacity—this has been notice-
able for several years—is not on a par with the nobility of his scruples.

MAY 28TH

When the radio announced early this morning
that the Prime Minister would broadcast at eight-
thirty, everyone knew that he was about to announce
an important piece of bad news. And so it was:
Reynaud, in somewhat melodramatic style, told the
country of King Leopold's "treason," that is, the
King's decision to accept unconditional surrender
to the enemy. In the afternoon, Churchill also spoke
of this event before the House of Commons, but without laying too heavy an accusation on the sovereign.
The Belgian ministers confined themselves to the
statement that the King's act was unconstitutional
and that he had decided upon it three days before.
This evening a crêpe veil was placed over the statue
of King Albert the First on the Place de la Concorde,
and men wept. But the defeat in the North seems
so important that everyone understands that it cannot be explained by the unfortunate decision of
one man, nor be accounted for by one episode, no
matter how dramatic. The remark most often heard
in connection with the King's capitulation is simply
this: "How lucky those Nazis are! Everything con-
tributes to their success. . . ." And a sort of fatality
bows all heads; it is as though people were already
resigned to the irreparable. And this beyond any

doubt is more grave than anything else. Nothing, or almost nothing, has been done to prevent people from drifting into this most pernicious attitude of discouragement. What the Minister of Information has done to arrest the ebbing of public morale does not count. The Radio Journal of France, in particular, has so ineffectually gained the country's attention that members of the most diverse social classes turn it off as soon as it begins a broadcast. There is no one who talks to the French in language that is suited to them. (Reynaud plays the part of the bearer of ill tidings, only.) From the very start of the "phoney war" the soldiers found themselves already in almost complete moral solitude, but today, when the call to arms should be sounded, it is much worse. And who, anyway, could sound the call to arms? No one would think of asking the Head of the Republic to address his fellow citizens. . . . The Commander in Chief has other things to do but speak. So, no Frenchman hears the voice of France; it is as though the Fatherland had lost its voice or become dumb. And this is the result of a long process by which the strong personalities have all been carefully prevented from reaching the front ranks . . . to this have all our labors led us. Rarely in our history has France been prevented from being conscious of herself, rarely incapable of being incarnated in some living person.

Saw Campinchi,[1] on business regarding my department, at the Ministry of the Navy. It seems that several important units of our fleet are working

1 Secretary of State for the Navy.

with the British before Calais and Dunkerque. The Minister of the Navy talks about the situation and describes what is happening up there, showing the map of operations in his office, and repeats several times in conclusion: "Oh, no, Blanchard's Army is not having a good time!" (General Blanchard commands the severed sections of the Army of the North. General Prioux is at the head of the French imprisoned in the pocket cut off from the other armies by the Germans.)

JUNE 1ST

It appears more and more clearly that Reynaud is pursuing two parallel policies: in his speeches he advocates resisting to the bitter end, but does not always act accordingly. And at times, he seems to follow a course of his own, a sort of personal diplomacy, which he is careful not to reveal to ambassadors.

The evacuation through Dunkerque is shaping up better than was thought, that is, in spite of the violence of the German assault, the intrenched camp resists heroically and protects the embarking troops far more effectively than one dared hope. There will be fewer men taken prisoner than was expected, and we are helped by favorable weather. The Supreme Council met yesterday in Paris. It does not seem probable that the British who have been shipped to England will return to France, for it is not yet known how the military situation will evolve. It is repeated that we will hold the Somme River, that if need be we will take up a stand on the Seine. But in this case, what will become of Paris? . . . Reynaud's immediate circle has its own ideas, but the Commander in Chief tells quite a different tale which the Prime Minister refuses to listen to.

At the meeting of the "Belgian Parliament" which was held at Limoges, about one hundred and fifty deputies and senators were assembled, but what is not told is that a larger number has remained in Belgium. Doubtless there will be two Belgiums, one with the King, the other in exile, and one can imagine the advantage to be derived from this situation by the Germans. . . . The German principles are neither complicated nor new, for they are the old, eternal recipes: "Divide and rule," etc. . . . They tried them out one by one on us, and we allowed it to go on without offering any more resistance than guinea pigs. They experimented on us, that is what they did, like a doctor on guinea pigs; they watched our reactions, experimented again; in short, they took a great deal of "interest" in *us,* who never took that sort of "interest" in *them.* Evidently a democracy is by definition *a country which is not interested in its neighbor,* which is in no way covetous; in itself this is excellent. It would be perfect if all countries were democracies.

But—and this is something we had never been warned of—it suffices that *one* partner in Europe adopt an ideology of war and conquest, for the game to be no longer equal or well balanced. The democracies must then either allow themselves little by little to be enslaved—that is, follow an appeasement policy—or decree a "moratorium of democracy," and fight with arms and methods capable of defeating the adversary's.

The tragedy lies in this, that when the fight becomes "serious," as it is at present, this "moratorium of democracy" is fatally forced upon the democracies. In England, since May 22d, the Government has had the right to commandeer at will possessions, resources and men. Can the Emergency Power Act voted by the Parliament be considered anything but a "moratorium of democracy"? In our country, likewise, since the military defeats in Belgium and in the North of France our Parliament has been, one might say, reduced to the brilliancy of a night light. The whole thing is to know whether this voluntary interruption of parliamentary authority, when it is determined upon *in extremis,* can still save the country.

France and England in recent years have been like two individuals who thought that it was quite unworthy of a civilized being to call in the firemen when the house was blazing, for firemen are people who use brutal methods. Germany has surreptitiously set the house afire in all sorts of hidden places, and at the same time she has insisted that a general conflagration would not consume our dwelling, and that the few flames visible would be extinguished of themselves, if we consented merely to get rid of this wardrobe, then of this piano and then of this table. . . . Finally France and England refused one day to be dispossessed of any more of their furniture and declared that there was a fire and that it had been caused by Germany. . . . And suddenly the whole thing burst into flames and it was only after the "House of France" found itself completely surrounded by fire and smoke that she decided to send in haste for the firemen.

JUNE 3D

I had just left the Ministry of Information, around half past one, when the sirens sounded; so I went to a little restaurant in a neighboring street, where lunch was still being served to customers. A uniform droning soon filled the sky, though not in the least bit deafening, and many sounds of explosions were heard in the distance; but most of the customers took them for the firing of anti-aircraft guns. On returning to my office I learned that Paris had been bombed in good earnest for the first time, that about two hundred and forty bombers had been over the capital. The raid is said to have taken six hundred victims. A few minutes later a thousand rumors were in circulation; it was said that the Citroen factories had been hit as well as the Air Ministry (where Mr. Bullitt had escaped a projectile by the merest chance). This evening I went along the Seine; at several points in the Citroen factories, some ruined bits still were smoking, but the damage does not seem too serious. Further on, near the Aviation Ministry, I saw great shell holes, two burnt motor-cars in the street and alongside almost every window pieces of broken glass. The crowd wandered about silently, and here again I suffered a bad impression: resignation prevailed. It would have been natural, however, that on the evening of the first day in which their beloved capital had been touched, Parisians should yield to a moment of anger and express a desire for revenge. But the looks on their faces seemed especially to say: "How the devil will all this end?" That a people as impulsive and quick as the French should have come to this can only signify that its resolution has been slowly sapping for years under the poisons of German propaganda. By a thousand means they have been made to feel disgust at the idea of "hitting out hard" against an eventual adversary; they have been terrified by the prospect of air bombings and an apocalyptical war. . . . A "pretty" piece of work has been accomplished with perfect impunity: our principles of liberty have been turned against us and have allowed our enemies every latitude in harming us on our own soil as much as they wish.

JUNE 4TH

Admiral Abrial was the last to leave the shores of Dunkerque, and more than four-fifths of the troops have been evacuated; this is beyond the most sanguine forecasts. However, Churchill has had the courage to tell the House of Commons that "wars are not won by evacuations." The Nazis began their great offensive only twenty-four days ago.

In deciding to reduce the pocket in the North, the Germans evidently wished to rid themselves of the latent menace during a march on Paris constituted by the Army of the North. And no doubt they also wished to separate France from England militarily, and this is all but accomplished. Only one British division remains on French soil. With the forced departure of the British Expeditionary Force we have lost ten British divisions and, what is more, much first-class war materiel. All this, added to the hundreds of thousands of soldiers taken by the Germans, the disappearance of the Belgian Army and our own losses in materiel, constitutes a great victory for the enemy. Over a thousand German planes seem to have been destroyed, while we are said to have lost two hundred and fifty planes ourselves. But two hundred and fifty machines mean a greater loss for us than a thousand planes to Goering.

Reynaud attempts to persuade the Senate that he has done everything to forestall the menace, which grows better defined day by day, from the Fascist Government. Indeed the Prime Minister's former "anti-Italian attitude" is a present reproach, but it is certain that during the last month the Government has been far more conciliatory to Italy—and this only encourages the aggressor of the eleventh hour.

Hélène de Portes maintains that "we must come to an understanding with Italy," which, under the circumstances, scarcely means anything. She has been most depressed by the news of the military disasters and, going from one extreme to the other, has all at once ceased to be the partisan of the "fight to the death" policy as she was a month ago. But how long will this new mood last? The same shrill laugh as before interrupts her words, but a most singular expression of nervous tension is to be seen on her face. At times, her glance is that of a hunted woman.

JUNE 5TH

Mandel received me today at his office. He allows it to be understood that more energetic decisions should have been taken by the Prime Minister, and that the mass of the people were expecting sanctions against those who have led us into our present fix.

"People don't see why those responsible for present events have not been designated." Naturally, this invites us to take the exact measure of Reynaud in the light of recent occurrences. . . . The military disasters gave the Prime Minister the sole advantage of using as much authority as he wished. But he has not *dared,* any more than he dared when he became Prime Minister on March 21st, at once to undertake something great. . . .

The case of Clemenceau—a politician who had kept fresh the temperament of a man of action—was quite exceptional, as we realize today. Our so-called "strong men" of today are swaying reeds. So the hardihood of ideas and decisions which Reynaud attributes to himself and which he had convinced us of, is no more than a borrowed cloak. . . . Would Mandel have been bolder? It is difficult to say for it is always easy for one of the opposition to play the part of the man of grim determination. On the other hand, because he is a Jew, Mandel would have had to steer an even more cautious course than others, and placate many people. . . . Some people say that Mandel is to Reynaud what Reynaud was to Daladier—but this remains to be proved.

Our own generation used to congratulate itself on the fact that there were only small men at the head of the government, for great men (and we were proud of this idea) can end by costing their countries very dear. . . . But since the Anti-Christ of democracy has sprung up in Berlin it must be realized that the charming, inefficient chatterboxes of our democracy will not be the ones to lay him low.

Several publicists of the extreme right, two of whom exercised their talents in the snobbish circles so skilfully corroded by Hitlerian Germany during the last five years, have been arrested.

In his Order of the Day, Weygand announces that the Battle of France is about to begin, and he exhorts all combatants to look "forward" only. The uninterrupted retreat has certainly demoralized the Army, which keenly feels, as does the rear, that there is no place to make a stand. The two adversaries do not follow the same conventions; we are like checker players who are familiar only with this game and are suddenly forced to play chess.

Before resolving to telephone directly to President Roosevelt, Reynaud listened to the objections that were raised, but decided to do it just the same. They attempted to show him that this unusual proceeding would be useless, that it was also useless to ask for planes, as the thousands of machines needed did not exist. This was reason enough. . . . On the other hand, the President of the United States could not thus distribute his country's planes, as though he were being asked to lend a dozen silver teaspoons belonging to the White House. . . . In short, this telephone call can only be like thrusting at thin air. . . . Reynaud is evidently so crushed by events that he feels that everything must be tried, and that he cannot be reproached for not having tried everything in his power.

The news of the day has been particularly discouraging, for we are told that the Weygand Line, hastily improvised, is not solid. . . . How lucky the

English are to have the Channel between them and
the invaders.... However, having opened a little book
a few minutes ago, I take on fresh courage. It is
made up of the notes written at the front this winter
by André Chamson and published under the title
Quatre Mois. The volume contains thoughts which
will perhaps prove in the long run more powerful
than events, whatever they may be: "This war is
perhaps nothing else but Europe's War of Secession.
The last convulsion before Europe is made. But
before she can be made, she might destroy herself.
She might destroy herself at the very moment her
historical fates insist that she should make herself.
. . . One fact alone remains certain: Europe cannot
be built on the excess power and the will to pre-
dominate in one of its parts—more exactly, in Germany. Our business is to prune this excess power.
But will we make Europe?" Perhaps a German victory (if one dares consider this hypothesis) would
be only a step backwards, never to happen again,
and that Europe will be made anyway. But are we
going to help make her?

Before France plays her part in this great enterprise she will have to make herself over, and Chamson, although he is on very good terms with men
in office and has worked by Daladier's side, has no
doubts whatever on this subject. (It is highly significant that not a single intelligent man *in any party*
has ever, during the last ten years, placed his faith
in the regime as it functions at present.) Here are
his reflections: "Hierarchy of office, fraternity of in-
tercourse, equality of destinies: the fate which pre-

sides over us at present is directing us towards this. . . ." And again: "These last two days I have seen too many men and too much distress. . . . To talk about these men, it would be necessary to discuss each one individually. However, I have one thing to say: Since this morning I have understood why the celebrated formula, 'united as at the front,' which was so often repeated in political parties between 1918 and 1939, has never been anything but a dead formula for twenty years. . . . Not that it is a false one, for once more it has revealed itself to be true. Between men and officers in infantry regiments I have seen complete fraternity. But this union, this fraternity, reposes upon the equality of destinies. In regiments of the line, soldiers and chiefs are in the same mud, the same danger. All social injustice has disappeared, or rather, men and officers live under the same injustice. There, to speak of union and fraternity means to answer the noblest, simplest and most direct movements of the human heart. But to make an appeal for fraternity when the inequality of destinies is reborn in peace, is to turn a great thing from its initial meaning. . . . This fraternity has meaning only in that equality of destinies which would subsist in peace as in war. Equality. Fraternity. . . . It is the first alone which makes the second possible. We must remember this. . . ." A few years ago a statistical inquiry was made, calling for some figure ranging from 1 to 100 to be chosen to designate in what measure Liberty, Equality and Fraternity were practised in our country. One of the answers read: Liberty, 99%; Equality, 75%; Fraternity, 5%.

. . . And this is true, that what we lacked most in peace time was this fraternity, which in war time spontaneously blooms again in the terrible climate of the front.

JUNE 6TH

Another ministerial reshuffling; Prouvost becomes Minister of Information, Reynaud having first said to him: "I commandeer you." Began to work as Prouvost's chief of staff [1] for foreign departments, as though the future were secure. . . . Reynaud has spoken once more on the radio and it seemed that he replied to the remark Mandel made the other day: he is not enquiring into questions of responsibility, he said, in order not to arouse controversies which would weaken France at a time when she needs union, etc. . . . At first this sounds very sensible, but if such a principle had been followed during the French Revolution, the Revolution would never have triumphed over its enemies.

The military news continues bad, and has now been so for such a long time that one cannot become any more discouraged: there is a limit to pessimism, and once a glimpse of the worst has been afforded, no further step down can be taken. However, the changes that a catastrophe would entail are so con-

[1] *Chef de cabinet.*

siderable that the mind cannot handle them and
doubts whether they can happen, although nothing
has appeared that will stop them. . . . It is **exactly**
the same as when a doctor tells you that a person
you love is dying, that there is no hope. Your reason
whispers that all is over, because a physician has
pronounced judgment, but at the same time someone within you passionately denies the possibility
of such an astounding misfortune.

It is said repeatedly, in the press and over the
air, that a new method has been found to arrest the
German advance: we are not to try establishing a
continuous line of resistance, as was done during the
last war, but are going to form "islands of resistance"
in quincunxes. The German tanks could advance a
certain number of kilometers but would finally be
annihilated by one group of resistance or the other.

Motor cars leave Paris filled with suitcases, furniture, boxes, parcels of all sorts. However, the restaurants in the center of Paris still keep up a certain
animation. On the Place de la Concorde and in the
middle of wide avenues, stakes and pylons are scat-
tered about to prevent enemy planes from landing,
and for the same reason old trucks have been massed
here and there. . . . The refugees arrive at the stations by thousands, with the horror of slaughter still
fresh in their memories, and many, as soon as they
find themselves in safety, give in to a nervous break-
down. . . . It seems as though fate had said to all
these good country people: "You were attached to
the goods of this world, you loved your houses and
fields? Well, you will leave all this at an hour's no-

tice and you will take to the road with a few clothes wrapped in a sheet, and that will be your all."

Reynaud has made Baudoin Under Secretary of State for Foreign Affairs and de Gaulle Under Secretary of State for War: one step towards peace and one towards total war.

The sentry at the Ministry of Information is not very much worried: his fortune-teller told him that France would finally be saved by a man who limps and that Hitler will be annihilated by "birds coming from the West."

JUNE 8TH

———◆●◆———

Today, a certain name has taken on a most lugubrious sound: Forges-les-Eaux. People repeat: "The Germans are at Forges-les-Eaux." It suddenly became clear that the Germans would soon reach Rouen and would cross the Seine, that the Battle of the Somme was already lost and that a "crystallizing" of the front was impossible at any point. The enemy marches in orderly formation with all its communications assured, and continually throws fresh troops into the battle. All this while we are dislocated, pressed back in disorder and without enough *reserves at our disposal*. This lack of men is the result of the absence of any birthrate policy in our country for the last fifty years, in spite of the warnings given by statistics and the steadily declining curve of births: for all mistakes must be paid for, one by one.

Went to General Headquarters at Vincennes with Prouvost, who had an appointment with General Weygand. In his vaulted office, the general spoke about the situation with the greatest calm, and yet this situation from his own admission is tragic. No pomp or ostentation surrounds him; a plain piece of matting is thrown over the cement flooring, as might be done in the hut of a modest colonial official. . . . No importunate telephone; officers come and go quietly from one room to the other, as though they were bringing in reports in peace time. The Commander in Chief's attitude is most comforting, but his words leave little ground for hope. We expect to be evacuated from Paris at any moment and it seems that the Government has shown itself most imprudent in not deciding to leave the city earlier.

JUNE 9TH

The fighting continues still; Weygand has published an Order of the Day saying that we must hold on one quarter of an hour longer than the enemy and that the Germans have suffered such considerable losses that their effort cannot be prolonged with the same intensity for very long. . . . But a miracle would indeed be necessary to prevent the foe from reaching Paris, when he is now at Gisors and at another point has crossed the river Aisne. Neutral journalists ask certain questions as a matter of form, and they are answered equally as a matter of form, but it is evident that they realize the situation. And they doubtless guess that we too know the situation: even if they believed the statements that we are ordered to make, one glance at our faces would make them realize the truth. . . . The German attack at Rethel is extremely violent and it is reckoned that three thousand enemy tanks are engaged in the offensive. The Ministry of Information, like the rest of the Administration, has received orders to pack up and go. All this passes human belief, extravagance mingles with horror as the quality of nightmare and magic intensify, together with an element of unreality.

Hélène de Portes, "on behalf of the Prime Minister," came here to announce to the Minister of Information what arrangements have been made: Paris will be considered an open town and put under the safeguard of Mr. Bullitt until the invader's arrival. The Prefect of Police, Langeron, will remain in the capital, as will the American Ambassador, and Mr. Biddle will follow the French Government to Tours so that another representative of the United States will be in permanent contact with Reynaud.

JUNE 10TH

Italy has declared war on us: this event is scarcely noticed by the populace, who do not consider it the most important event of the moment. As usual, Reynaud announced this piece of bad news in a broadcast: before his harangue (which was a little too melodramatic for my taste) the first notes of the chorus of the *Marseillaise* indicated that he spoke from a State station.

Filled the last bags with the last bundles of papers and the typewriters, at the Ministry. From today on our services are practically paralyzed: the documents go in one direction, the functionaries in another, and so it is with the entire Administration. In short, the brain of the administrative machine works only partially: yet another advantage for the enemy. Telephoned a friend who lost his mother a short while ago; he had always lived with her in Paris. I asked him if he was leaving the city and he replied, almost angrily: "What for? I care only for my memories, my memories are here, so here I stay and I don't care what happens to me." This determination is all the more remarkable as this friend bears a name that must necessarily attract the invader's notice.

When I told the housemaid that she could go back

to her family in the country at once if she wished, she smiled: "I'm in no hurry. And then I won't leave before putting the house in order for the summer. . . ." She did not believe in the arrival of the Germans, in spite of the rumors that fill our quarter, and she takes me to be a bit of a defeatist. . . . One of the things which have harmed us most in these last few years is what was called our "magnificent optimism," our conviction that "that" could not happen in our country. France also said: "I'm in no hurry. . . . Let me first put the house in order."

At nine o'clock in the evening, a comrade said to me: "Let's go and eat something" . . . (we had had no lunch). But where to go? We left the Ministry and found the Rue de Rivoli and the Rue de Castiglione completely deserted. At the same time, we noticed with amazement that great dark clouds of vapor obscured the air, putting halos around the street lights like those in a London fog in December. What could this mean? Could there be a great fire near Paris?

We reached the Ritz and went in, on the chance of finding a meal. A fantastic sight awaited us: The completely empty hall was faintly outlined by a feeble greenish light. Tonight was the first time that the Ritz had believed in the reality of the war, and it had concealed its lights in order to create a real blackout. The ghost of a head waiter glided between the shades of the waiters. In the restaurant one sees through a sort of milky haze four pieces of human wreckage, the four last customers. Thousands and thousands of tourists and society people who have reigned here, who have caught the tone of the smart set, or who thought to impart it, have sent none of their own delegates tonight. The four diners who close the list (which will not appear in the society column of the *Figaro*) are a journalist and his wife, the Prefect of Police and his wife. The two last witnesses will be the representative of order and the reporter. The only question everyone asks is this: How is Reynaud going to get out of this, as the game, militarily speaking, is lost? All this conversation among guests who stare at each other in the glaucous lighting, which makes the room look like the bottom of the sea, sounds like sentences uttered in a dream. . . . One of the hotel guests explained the specks of soot which envelop the city like a crêpe veil: "The Germans, to cross the Seine, made a great quantity of artificial clouds and the wind has blown this dirty smoke over Paris. . . ." So the "phenomenon" is very easy to understand. And so one thinks, in spite of oneself, of "the signs in the heavens" which poets—and the people—discover when some fabulous event is about to take place. . . . As I write these lines, the order comes to rejoin our cars for departure (it is eleven o'clock at night). The office that I am leaving will no doubt be occupied by the Germans in one day.

JUNE 11TH

The journey from Paris to Tours transcends all imagination. A famous foreign journalist said to me: "For the last twenty years I have always been sent by my paper to places where things were going badly; I have hunted tragedy like game, here and there all over Europe. I have witnessed I don't know how many wars and revolutions. . . . Well, I have never seen anything to equal the Biblical exodus of the Paris population."

So we left last night around eleven o'clock, and as our cars were to follow upon one another, the speed of the caravan was most moderate. In the suburbs we drove like a funeral procession, for the roads were blocked with vehicles in close succession or, to be more accurate, were pressing one another on. And all these cars were disfigured, so to speak, with monstrous excrescences of mattresses on their tops, of bicycles attached to their hoods or children's carriages hanging from the back. . . . Bicycle riders were passing alongside the cars, with little bundles tied to the handlebars; and there were old men on foot with bags on their backs. After Sceaux we were stopped continually by barricades and our convoy dispersed. My car refused to go on: and so I suddenly found myself, with no headlights, before an inn; it was

about two in the morning and other cars were
ranged in disorder all around. One would take it
to be a vast disorderly encampment improvised in
the darkness, a sort of mysterious rendezvous in
deep shadow. . . . By dawn I had repaired my car as
best I could, and was then able to see that there
were a number of other cars about me which had
broken down, and still others which had rolled
into the ditches at the sides of the road. There were
a great many accidents caused by drivers who had
not dared turn on their headlights for fear of being
bombed.

In the vicinity of most villages, the road was barred
for about four-fifths of its width by tree trunks,
mountains of great stones, rails and bits of beams
covered over with branches. . . . Worn out by sleep-
less nights, but looking most resolute, Territorial
troops or peasants, guns slung over their shoulders,
were on the look-out for parachutists: they scanned
our faces and examined our papers minutely before
allowing us to pass. . . . Were these primitive barricades set up to arrest the progress of enemy tanks?
Peasant women, holding their children by the hand,
stood at a respectful distance from our procession,
stupefied at learning from the appearance of cars
covered with eiderdowns and comforters the ap-
proach of the catastrophe. . . . Just a few came up
to speak to us, and they asked in a timid voice:
"So it seems that things are not going at all well,
monsieur?"

Long before Tours it was almost impossible to
advance, and it seemed from afar that not a car was

moving on the interminable bridge that spans the Loire. The populace looked at the rows of cars with expressions not without reprobation. To the inhabitants of Touraine, who were in favor of decent behavior, these horrible-looking cars were rather shocking.

As soon as we were settled at the "Institut de Touraine," we discovered that nothing had been sufficiently well organized ahead of time to allow the immediate resumption of work. The Ministry of Information was obliged to spend its time collecting . . . information concerning the other ministries. Where was the Ministry of the Navy? Is General Headquarters really at Briare? The whereabouts of the Prime Ministry were known, but the President of the Republic appeared to have been forgotten in some pitfall. And what a strange idea, anyway, to have fallen back on Tours, which is so near Paris! An unimaginative functionary must have chosen this place of retreat for the Government—as though conditions of modern warfare were the same as in 1870. Situated only 230 kilometers from Paris and very accessible, Tours is an inexplicable choice. And as there are too few public buildings which can be utilized, the result is that a single ministry is often cut into two or three sections.

Yesterday Reynaud telephoned once more to the President of the United States, to whom he had also sent a message. But publication of this message has been delayed in the press because it would be desirable to publish the answer at the same time as the request. Churchill came to Tours by air and Rey-

naud tried to make it plain that the game seemed lost
for us from a military point of view. Several members of the Cabinet think that there is nothing left
to do now but to solicit an armistice and to ask England to release us from the obligation we had taken
not to conclude a separate peace. . . . At the same
time, however, the Government and the Command
continue to ask the Information to soften the gravity
of the news in presenting it to the people.

In the High Street of Tours is a succession of the
most unexpected persons: the Cardinal Archbishop
of Paris, a member of the Comédie-Française, ministers, bankers, etc. . . . It is a lugubrious caricature
of the smart "season," a sort of tragic Salzburg. But
the well-known men and the others who are not well-
known all have another face—I might say a second
face—and sometimes it is difficult to recognize their
features under the mask of anguish that overlies
them. There is a sort of "make-up" of sorrow. At
the "Hôtel de l'Univers," which passes for the best in
town, one is surprised to meet flotsam and jetsam
from the Senate and Chamber. Most of the politicians who for years have been "reassuring" the
country and living on the lies they told it, had been
there for two days, broken down, like clandestine
traffickers in drugs whose shameful trade had been
at last discovered. One of the senators is so deaf that
the last pieces of bad news had to be roared in his
ear—and the truth finally reached him.

JUNE 12TH

The Germans are at Reims and it is thought that they will enter Paris tomorrow morning; millions of Parisians have left the capital. The Cabinet meetings are held almost continuously but no one dares to draw any definite conclusions from this. Today at Cangé, at the meeting of the Council of Ministers, General Weygand declared that there was nothing left to do but to ask for an armistice. . . . Reynaud is going to ask the British who have just left him, to come back to confer with him.

A chance billeting sends me to lodge at La Bechellerie, the house where Anatole France used to live. And here again, the same feeling of unreality pursues me. It is indeed curious at the present moment to enter a museum-house such as this one, where the sweetness of the eighteenth century still remains imprisoned in walls delightfully covered with old damask and adorned with charming drawings of the period. . . . We expect to be bombed at any moment by the Germans who, according to an intercepted message, seem to intend raiding the provisional capital of the French Government, so as to frighten the ministers and hasten the hour of capitulation. . . . The owners of La Bechellerie scan the sky anxiously, the sky which their great-uncle Anatole France always looked upon with a smiling face. . . . On the other side of the road lives Henri Bergson: the philosopher has refused to leave his estate and will remain there, no matter what happens. The memory of Anatole France, the person of Bergson, the old silks and precious furniture which adorn the house of the first, the books and manuscripts which fill the house of the second: between these and the Panzer divisions, nothing remains. What a significant contrast! The nation which produced Bergson and France has not been able adequately to protect herself against the inferior tribes who dream only of conquest. Our nation was too much interested in Bergson and France and their like, that is, in civilization. . . . Hélène de Portes now sobs and begs Reynaud to resign. . . . I was told only today that she attempted to burst in upon the Supreme Council during one of the sessions. An officer kept her from entering, and she slapped him.

JUNE 13TH

Last night I was leaving the Hôtel de l'Univers (where, as every place else, one must now wait an hour before obtaining half a meal) when the sirens sounded. I struck a match to see which house I could enter for refuge and thereupon barely escaped being bludgeoned: "Lights! Lights!" cried voices in the darkness; my box of matches was torn from my hand and no doubt it was thought that I was about to signal enemy planes. I groped my way back to the hotel where the whistling sound of bombs was heard rather distinctly. In the hall a young woman, prone on a sofa, was asked to go down to the cellar. But she did not move an eyelash, much less a finger. "She came here before dinner," the hotelkeeper said to me, "staggering with fatigue, and at once fell into her present state of prostration. She does not answer when spoken to and it is quite clear that she does not even understand what is said to her." She was transported carefully to the cellar, where she tumbled at once onto the chair that was given her.

A curious fact, which I have noticed all around me, is that people *no longer ask for news,* are tired of listening to the radio and the opening bars of the *Marseillaise* chorus which precede the announcement of disasters. These people are no longer interested in anything but their neighbors, and they help one another, they attempt to solve the questions that have supplanted war problems: the question of lodgings, of food, of finding out where to send children, etc. . . . This is the "equality of destinies" which existed at the front and which now concerns civilians, too, who have been chased from their homes. Perhaps we are too much taken with appearances, and because we have lost our homes we wrongly think that we have lost everything. It is indeed terrible to abandon one's house, one's city . . . but sorrow also has another *side:* this total impoverishment can enrich us, we can *gain,* for example, this very fraternity between Frenchmen which is now manifested everywhere. . . .

After a fresh interview with Churchill (who also saw Mandel) Reynaud explained to the English the motives which impelled France to do nothing beyond asking for an armistice; at the same time he delayed the final decision for twenty-four hours, he said, in order to know President Roosevelt's answer. Tonight, Reynaud in a brief broadcast indicated that he had made a last and pressing appeal to America for "clouds of planes." . . . The present situation cannot last long: one hundred and twenty German divisions are marching between Rouen and the Maginot Line. Politicians will now be forced out of their ambiguous stand. . . . It is said that Reynaud tried to persuade Churchill to sue for an armistice, too, but in vain.

A nurse who returned here with a convoy of automobile ambulances made some remarks which tallied exactly with the thoughts of many of us. Her words came as a surprise, for they were spoken by a woman who in peace time lived the most artificial of lives. Rich and snobbish, so worldly that her permanent address was Vanity Fair, her delicate hands and painted nails seemed made solely to finger precious jewels. Today I looked at her hands, which had become tough and almost callous from driving a heavy car over broken roads for days and nights. Her face was unpainted and no longer pretty; it was beautiful because humanity appeared there for the first time. We questioned this nurse, our friend, for a long time; she has been through a hell and has learnt a great deal: "Beyond a certain degree of moral suffering," she said, "you feel that nothing more can touch you, and something that must be called serenity blends with your sorrow. An obscure sensation of liberation comes over you, once you know that you are no longer vulnerable. . . ." She continued: "The hardest part of a great trial is the *novelty* of it, which suddenly changes everything . . . but once your soul is accustomed to the knowledge that the house has burnt down, that the war is lost, that Paris will be occupied . . . then your soul reaches another region which is certainly not one of happiness, but neither is it one of surpassing grief: it can be called a region which is above sorrow. After that, there remains one more stage to travel: to find in the complete forgetfulness of oneself the exaltation necessary for true devotion to fellow-creatures." This woman must have seen much suffering around her and must have suffered a great deal herself to have arrived at such a clear perception of spiritual realities. . . . Everyone, no matter how small his part in the ordeals which crush the country, has had a glimpse, like the nurse who spoke to us a few moments ago, of a new spiritual world revealed vaguely, like a landscape fitfully lit up by a conflagration. Someone has just come to Tours from the north of France where he beheld the destruction of his château by bombs. Before the catastrophe, he was the most miserly man I had ever met. Yesterday he admitted: "In peace time, I was furious, almost sick when a servant broke a vase—

well, only a fortnight ago I left my house in ruins
and I don't give it a thought. . . ."

The nurse added a remark which is worth noting:
"There have been moments," she said, "when after
seeing what the French are capable of doing for one
another in their present distress, *I have been tempted
to thank Hitler.*"

In the hours we are now living through, the most
commonplace meetings can become fascinating. This
morning I wanted to have my car repaired and all
the big garages were overwhelmed with work, so I
was obliged to ask the services of a small artisan. I
reached Berthelin's shop—that was the artisan's name
—to find his wife knitting peacefully in a corner of
the office and the apprentice busying himself in the
workshop. Berthelin at once understood what to do,
told me to come back in a couple of hours and I
would find the car repaired. I was lucky enough to
find two new tires, which are a rarity at present.
When Berthelin left the shop for a moment, the
apprentice said to me, speaking of his master with
wondering admiration: "And you know, he's been
at it again!" So I enquired of Berthelin what he had
done during the war and learnt that he had enlisted
in a regiment of armored tanks, although he had
been released from military obligations. And it was
only quite recently that he was sent back to his workshop, in the capacity of technician. During his stay
at the front, he advanced in his tank to a point where
some German infantry soldiers, taken by surprise,
resisted without hope of rescue. Most of them fell at

once under our fire, without retreating an inch: "They were really amazing fellows," said Berthelin, "but when I closed in on the last one, I saw his face and his expression just before he fell: an empty face, eyes without a trace of expression, and I understood that this hero was above all a poor guy. . . ." Berthelin then spoke at great length of the Germans, always with great dignity and also very shrewdly. He told me, as many other soldiers have done: "If only they would let us live peacefully in our country. . . . We haven't anything against those people. . . ." And unwittingly echoing Paul Valéry, this philosopher in blue overalls concluded: "Men are mad with stupidity." But instead of "stupidity," he used a livelier term.

When I was ready to leave his shop, Berthelin refused my tip, and for the new tires charged me according to an old price list, which was as good as making me a present. He belongs to the race of peasants sung by Péguy: It is not money that attracts him above all things else, but rather the satisfaction derived from "perfect work," and what he seeks from life is the chance to remain a free artisan. "The big boys," he explained to me (meaning the men who have created a garage trust in this region) "have tried to break me because I don't cheat customers, but so far, I've been able to hold my own. . . ." Berthelin awaits with the greatest calm the arrival of the Germans: "Because after all, once they're here, what can they do?" he asked me with a half smile. Men like Berthelin cannot be changed by circumstances —and France produces a lot of Berthelins, a lot of

individuals who have not been made on the wholesale plan.

This Thursday evening, in the ill-lit room where
the Minister camps and where the only radio set is
to be found that has survived our wanderings, sits
Eve Curie. She came to hear the radio news. Once
more we listened to the first few bars of the *Marseillaise* and then, as usual, to very bad news. We
talked of other things, we pretended afterwards to be
absorbed in a thousand insignificant tasks, but there
were ill-concealed tears in many eyes, not only in Eve
Curie's but in the eyes of several officers who were
present. The French Army, which still amounted to
forty-six divisions ten days ago, consists now of only
twenty-four divisions. The Germans have about one
hundred and twenty-five divisions.

JUNE 14TH

They have entered Paris.

Today we have received orders to leave for Bordeaux at once. And once more the ministries wander
over the highroads. . . . This evacuation can have
but one meaning, we are told: it is but a stage in a
longer journey, doubtless to Africa, because it is
inconceivable now that French military resistance
can be organized at any point in the country with
any chance of success, considering the positions now

occupied by the enemy. On the other hand, the Maginot Line is about to be rounded. . . . And one's impression is that the Government flees from one town to the other without seeing any further than the end of its nose, and that it goes on putting off the moment for the supreme decision. This is not so much fleeing from the Germans as it is fleeing from responsibility.

The same procession of shabby cars as on the journey between Paris and Tours. We stopped for the night at Bellac and had not known that we were falling into a sort of Babel. In this little French town, as shut in and retiring as a little French town can be in peace time, we found Hollanders who had taken shelter here a few days before, Luxemburgers, Flemings—and Alsatians evacuated from Alsace in September, 1939. At the town hall people were at first surprised to . . . hear us speak French without an accent and we aroused suspicion when we asked for gasoline tickets and billets. . . . Finally we convinced the authorities of our good intentions and everything passed off most cordially.

In the high street the war has changed many things; it has stuck up signs in Flemish and Alsatian for the guests of the moment, but in the adjacent alleys we find the eternal tranquillity of the provinces, cats curled up on steps, a priest pedalling slowly by on his lady's bicycle, lace curtains mysteriously lifted after the passing of the "stranger," crusty loaves of bread shining in the baker's window. Children are playing with a pail; they lower it into a well, bring it up, empty it, etc. . . . And the creaking of the chain

on the windlass is a sound one cannot tire of; it
abolishes all bad memories for a time.

JUNE 15TH

———◆◆◆———

Arrival in Bordeaux. Same Judgment Day throng
as at Tours. Everybody begins to understand that
life is but a tragedy divided by more or less lengthy
intermissions. On the Place de la Comédie, the innumerable crowd resembles no crowd ever seen before: It is a crowd of players who have lost the game.
Tragedy, which we thought possible only in books,
has become the life of every day, and the best reporting of the fall of Paris is not to be found in
Paris-Soir but in the Bible, in the Lamentations of
Jeremiah: "How doth the city sit solitary, that was
full of people! How is she become as a widow! She
that was great among the nations, and princess among
the provinces, how is she become tributary!

"She weepeth sore in the night, and her tears are
on her cheeks: among all her lovers she has none
to comfort her. . . .

"And from the daughter of Zion all her beauty is
departed: her princes are become like harts that find
no pasture, and they are gone without strength before the pursuer. . . ."

All these "harts that find no pasture" and who
"are gone without strength before the pursuer" have

been here in Bordeaux for the last twenty-four hours, and some, as in the old days of junketing and spree- ing, go to dine at the "Chapon Fin." But faces are ghastly, and every guest has the expression of a con- demned man who has just been awakened and who knows that *the* day has come.

Most of the Parisian men and women who have come here are forced into a terrible choice. One woman has had to decide whether she would remain with her mother or rejoin her husband; a widow whom I met a moment ago has been obliged to give up following the man she loves and whom she is shortly to marry in order to stay with her children. . . . The bonds of blood or affection are tested by ordeals they have never known. It is impossible to conciliate matters as one would in peace time, to divide one's life and one's heart; decisions must be taken, preferences shown. . . . Those who think first of their worldly possessions cling to them, those who wish to preserve that most precious of all goods, liberty, see themselves in Africa, and are already im- agining what this separation from their native land will mean. In every case there are privations, sepa- rations, anguish, laceration. . . . Impossible to get around a dilemma now (as the whole country did for so many years, answering for instance, the alter- native: "Butter or cannons?" with "Butter *and* can- nons"). Fate puts questions which must be answered by yes or no, and one is certain of losing a great deal, if one does not lose all.

It is easy now to understand that life in peace time was founded on a great many compromises, on ingenious arrangements, on salutary lies; we see that this life had set up false exits and sham windows in perfect symmetry. . . . It was a skilful construction, whereby the most diverse forces formed an equilibrium, where everything had been conceived to avoid violence and economize pain. By closing our ears we feigned not to hear unpleasant truths, and the art of getting around difficulties and painful efforts did not subsist without a certain amount of hypocrisy. . . . Today the age of brutality has returned: now every man is forced to show on the spot what he thinks and what he is worth.

A naval officer who lives in this same sordid little hotel has just uttered a few melancholy words, words which sound rather insignificant, but which sum up a good deal: "We could never have believed things would come to this. . . ." He pursued his thought as follows: "We had certain ready-made ideas about peace, about war, about France, about Germany, but we did not think that events would take us at our word, that we would be called upon to give up everything, our possessions, our lives, to defend certain principles. . . . For years, for instance, the Hitlerian aggressions aroused our indignation and we were justly angry. However, when the question of dying for Prague arose, many of us in 1938 asked leave to think it over: our moral reprobation became as inadequate as a banknote that is refused when payments in gold are required. . . ."

It is true that many of the opinions which we adopt in happy times, and which, as we say, cost nothing, have but a relative value. These opinions are shared by millions of beings, but how many of them would die for such ideas? Many in this mass will not keep the same color when the hour has struck for the great ordeal, and there is no doubt but that in a moment of mortal danger the number of chameleons seriously rises in all countries. . . .

This is partly because our State has allowed its authority to vanish, little by little, and has not galvanized its energies in recent weeks. Indeed, the greater the impression of strength the State gives the more easily do citizens give it all their energy. . . . Our democracy does not rally all who should be rallied at present; but it would be otherwise if the democracy had been transformed into a Committee of Public Safety when circumstances demanded it. . . .

On the Place de la Comédie, an officer said confidentially to some friends: "Verdun is taken." A few minutes later, the news had gone around the café and filled everyone with dismay, not that the event is so serious in itself, but Verdun has symbolized so much since the last war. . . .

It seems that Gamelin, ever since he was relieved of his command, has been living in Paris and spends his time writing his own vindication. He repeats, in defence: "If General Joffre had been put on the shelf after the Charleroi retreat, there would never have been a victory on the Marne."

Another Cabinet meeting tonight under the presidency of Monsieur Lebrun; it was even longer than usual. One of the ministers remarked: "For all that, Reynaud will have to give birth to something." The British are becoming uneasy at these long, fruitless

debates. The Army can no longer fight, but the Fleet
is intact and several ways of settling its fate are discussed. Some would like the Fleet to be simply handed
over to England, others advise giving it to the United
States as "a gift made to the cause of liberty." Reynaud inclines to the last solution, but up to the present has not put his idea into execution.

JUNE 17TH

Marshal Pétain succeeded Reynaud as Prime
Minister last night. (He threatened to resign yesterday as Vice Premier if the Government did not ask
for an armistice.) This morning he announced in a
voice never to be forgotten by those who heard it,
that "fighting must cease." However, we received an
order to tell the press to offer a slightly different
version of the appeal; the *Petite Gironde* quoted the
Marshal in its columns as declaring that "an attempt
must be made to stop the fighting." This attenua-
tion has not prevented the spread of consternation
in the Bordelaise crowd. For the majority of the inhabitants of Bordeaux, in spite of the presence of
refugee Parisians, still were filled with illusions.
Silent groups of people and women in tears could
be seen before the newspaper stands.

Yesterday, the great step had to be taken. What
a day! I went to and fro—from the Havas Agency,

where the office of the Minister of Information camps, to the Rue Vital-Carles, where the Government sits almost continuously. The crowd, which is not very numerous, is held in by policemen, far off from the entrance gate, as people are kept at a respectful distance from an accident. During the last gubernatorial deliberations, three clans have been formed: the "hard" clan directed in principle by Reynaud and in fact by Mandel—for Reynaud always allows himself to be influenced by the arguments of the "soft." He recognized, however, that his earlier attitude prevented him from bowing to circumstances, and one could conclude from the way he expressed this thought that he was ready to "serve" the country . . . in another place. . . . Marin joined Mandel in the "hard" camp: so the Nazi reclassification of French political parties found its confirmation in the last ministerial councils of Bordeaux.[1] Marin, head of the Right party, has adopted the same attitude of resistance as Mandel—a minister often attacked by the right—while other right wing deputies voted with the Socialists for capitulation. . . . Between the two camps were the prudent ones. Dautry, in the course of a long discussion, brought about a long silence when he said: "It remains now for France to know whether she will steer towards the Anglo-Saxon world or towards the Germanic world."

President Roosevelt's answer being known, the

---

[1] Nazi reclassification of French political parties brings up the operation by which German propaganda had succeeded long before the war in cutting each party in two, and thereby substituting for the existing nineteen groups an occult system of two groups: The party for *appeasement* and that *against appeasement*.

moment to speak out could no longer be delayed, and Churchill's sensational proposal of "union between France and England" called for a reply. This surprising proposal showed great energy of imagination, and there was nothing to be said against it except that it had been made *in extremis*. Our democracies, which have been so gravely lacking in imagination, have invented something at the last moment—just as they built planes when they were in the last extremity: they do what they can, but their strategy is the snail's strategy. . . . One cannot help thinking, with bitter regrets, what such a "union" between our two countries would have meant after Munich, for instance . . . when the decisive moment came to vote, thirteen ministers rejected the proposal and there were ten votes in its favor.

Marshal Pétain has taken power to try and conclude an armistice at once. Still no one knows what will happen to the fleet, and it is a great pity that the Germans have not been shown a *fait accompli* before an armistice is called for. . . . However we are still told that we are to leave Bordeaux; soon, for the Germans will surely wish to settle down here. The Government would go for the time being to Perpignan, some say to Saint-Jean-de-Luz(?) before taking refuge perhaps in Africa.

This morning, before the Hotel Montré, met Hélène de Portes, She was so pale that I scarcely recognized her. And she immediately began a violent discourse: "We are going only because we have to, the President should not resign, etc. . . ." This was all the more surprising, since it had been said

in various quarters for some time that she insisted
on Reynaud's leaving his premiership at once. She
asked me what I thought of the "provisional departure of Reynaud"; I could answer nothing. The political downfall of a man whose intelligence I had
admired during the recent years, with whom I had
worked a little and in whose character I had placed
some hope, comes after so many disillusionments
that no one can regret it. It is Daladier *bis* who is
leaving.

Daladier, Reynaud, all these names are the various pseudonyms of the "average prime minister"
who has governed France for years, and whose true
name is Monsieur Pull-the-Wires. Monsieur Pull-
the-Wires has allowed the old school to rule the
Army and has chloroformed to the best of his ability
all Frenchmen susceptible of rising up before external peril. Ministries of the right have been formed
by Monsieur Pull-the-Wires, as well as ministries of
the left; and in 1936 there was an "advanced" ministry; it was a Pull-the-Wires like the others.

In the streets of Bordeaux, tonight, nothing is
talked about but traitors who ought to be shot, but
their names cannot be found. The most dangerous
traitors are not those who betrayed merely for
money, but the many who betrayed the interests of
France with their spirit of wire-pulling.

Impossible to remain seated before a café, Place
de la Comédie, tonight; we drifted there before dinner. Despair has become an element of the air, we
breathe it in like a poison; and what is more depressing than anything else is to hear what is said of

our last chance, England: "Alas, she can't hold out a month, for the Nazis will cross the Channel in July, etc. . . ." Met H. R. Knickerbocker: "The Germans will not win," he said to me. "It may take ten years but they will be beaten." Amen.

The End

INDEX